UNDERSTANDING PROGRAM EVALUATION

SAGE HUMAN SERVICES GUIDES, VOLUME 31

SAGE HUMAN SERVICES GUIDES

a series of books edited by ARMAND LAUFFER and published in cooperation with the University of Michigan School of Social Work.

A **SAGE** HUMAN SERVICES GUIDE 31

UNDERSTANDING PROGRAM EVALUATION

Leonard RUTMAN
George MOWBRAY

Published in cooperation with the University of Michigan School of Social Work

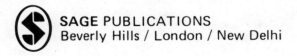

SAGE PUBLICATIONS
Beverly Hills / London / New Delhi

For information address:

SAGE Publications, Inc.
275 South Beverly Drive
Beverly Hills, California 90212

SAGE Publications India Pvt. Ltd.
C-236 Defence Colony
New Delhi 110 024, India

SAGE Publications Ltd
28 Banner Street
London EC1Y 8QE, England

Printed in the United States of America

Library of Congress Cataloging in Publication Data

Rutman, Leonard.
   Understanding program evaluation.

   (Sage human services guide, v. 31)
   "Published in cooperation with the University of Michigan School of Social Work."
   1. Evaluation research (Social action programs) 2. Social work administration.
I. Mowbray, George II. University of Michigan. School of Social Work. III. Title.
IV. Series: Sage human services guides ; v. 31.
HV11.R874   1983   361.3'068   83-4451
ISBN 0-8039-2093-8 (pbk.)

FIRST PRINTING

CONTENTS

PREFACE

Understanding Program Evaluation is a guidebook to better management through the use of program evaluation. It is directed to two primary audiences: (1) managers in charge of national, state, and local social programs, and (2) students who one day may become program managers or on occasion carry out evaluations under the general direction of such managers. For the students, and their instructors, the cases and questions in the Appendix at the back of the book provide guidance for planning and simulating evaluations.

We believe that the emphasis in this book on evaluation as a managerial tool for better program delivery fits the requirements of line managers. Evaluations will continue to be carried out for external accountability to funding and other oversight agencies, particularly in times of economic restraint. However, line managers are an important client for evaluations directed toward program improvement. Accountability evaluations ask a key question: Is the program any good? The managerial evaluation asks: How can the program be made better? We look on our emphasis as realistic. We have seen that "political" issues tend to outweigh evaluation findings when public policies are being made and fiscal priorities set. Too many external evaluations have had little impact. But internally directed ones have, we believe, considerable unexploited potential. They can and should offer practical advice to program managers. Our book is designed to both encourage and support such evaluations, to be more responsive to client needs and increase program effectiveness. This is all grist for the managerial mill.

For persons concerned about "accountability" — surely one of the fuzziest buzz words in current vogue — we suggest that the concept has two dimensions, one *external* and the other *internal*. Externally, the program manager and evaluators are required to account for the stewardship of public funds, to promote and defend the "ideas" on which the program is based (if they can be defended), and to play a role in the competition between worthy objects of public expenditure for increasingly scarce legislative appropriations. But internally, the manager is the apex of the accountability structure. He or she is the one to whom all program staff are "accountable" for the economy, efficiency, and effectiveness of program delivery. Evaluations can help strengthen this vitally important "internal accountability," and with it, the quality of program delivery.

—*L.R.*
G.M.
Ottawa

Chapter 1

UNDERSTANDING THE NATURE OF
PROGRAM EVALUATION

Program evaluation suffers from a duality of purpose, making its nature hard to understand in simple terms. On the one hand, evaluations called for by legislatures and funding agencies may imply, in part, questions of purpose, relevance, and financial priority. On the other, evaluations initiated by the program manager are likely to have largely internal audiences and internal aims related to improving — not shelving — the principal components of the program. Most programs exhibit remarkable staying power, so that even where evaluations are supposed to affect budgeting, major changes are not likely to flow from the evaluation as such. Other, more political factors typically have more influence on the eventual fate of policies and programs. Our view, therefore, is that the most practical nature of evaluation embodies a quest for better program delivery. Hence our management-oriented approach in this book.

BACKGROUND

Managers and students of public administration are the heirs of a long tradition in program evaluation. It is not new, even if it is more widely touted than ever before — with a mind-boggling roster of publications, texts, books of readings, journals, encyclopedias, and the yearly publication, *Evaluation Studies*. Program evaluation has become a profession and the subject of specialization in higher educational curriculums, but some views of more than a generation ago still echo today.

As early as 1908, C. C. Carstens wrote:

> It is only when the work of studying results is given a share of . . . time . . . that we can hope to defend the faith that is in us, or what is more likely to be the case, modify our theories in many important particulars, nay, build a new philosophy in a number of fields upon the sure foundation of facts.[1]

In 1923, the newly organized American Association of Social Workers established a Subcommittee on Evaluation to look into the literature on the subject. It reported that there "had been almost no attempt, either by organizations or individual workers, to evaluate the results of social casework."[2]

In his presidential address to the 1931 National Conference of Social Work, Richard Cabot exhorted social agencies to "make more of these fallible judgments, to expose themselves more often to the dangers of statistics, the risks which come to light when we announce and apply our criteria by which we believe our success or failure may be judged."[3] Dr. Cabot set out to meet his own standards by developing and financing the now-famous *Cambridge-Somerville Youth Study,* one of the first controlled experiments to evaluate the effectiveness of therapeutic interventions. The study, begun in 1939, tested the efficacy of using "big brother" counseling to reduce antisocial behavior among teenage predelinquent males. The study was completed by Edwin Powers and Helen Witmer and published in 1951.[4]

Girls at Vocational High was another classic study during this same period. In the mid-1950s, an experiment was designed to test the effectiveness of a preventive social work service to school girls defined as potentially delinquent.[5] About the same time, a study entitled *The Chemung County Evaluation of Casework Service to Multi-Problem Families* was reported.

The focus of this study was on the effectiveness of intensive case work with multiproblem families.[6]

Numerous other studies of social work intervention were reported in the late 1960s.[7] These studies represent an interest by professionals in learning about the effectiveness of their interventions. Most of the studies presented disappointing results. That is, programs were not producing a significant impact on the measured objectives relative to the situation of control groups who did not receive the services. Whether or not these findings were valid is not at issue here. (Later in the text, we will identify factors that help account for such findings.)

The mid-1960s saw evaluation being used to test prospective policies and programs on a pilot basis for possible future adoption. Demonstration projects were funded (e.g., guaranteed annual income experiments, Head Start and Follow Through, health insurance, and a variety of correctional services such as diversion experiments and restitution programs). Services were established along with the requirement that the effectiveness of what were innovative and new programs or interventions be measured. Findings could presumably then be used in deliberations about their long-term prospects.

In the current context, evaluation is viewed mainly as a medium of "accountability." The present situation has been described as follows:

> Thus, for many years, the human services operated beyond the pale of public scrutiny. In the past decade, however, the public's blind acceptance of professional assurances and government sponsorships has changed to a chary wariness, even suspiciousness, and evaluation schemata are being imposed on human service endeavors.[8]

Program evaluation is currently viewed as a tool for aiding decisions on cutting budgets of programs during the prevailing situation of economic constraint and inflation accompanied by large government deficits. Undoubtedly, many evaluations, analyses, and reviews will be done for this purpose. Yet the delivery of programs in an economic and efficient manner remains as a challenge. Evaluations that serve this purpose are what we are interested in here. This implies far more scope for program evaluation than what is required for simple "go/no go" decisions on basic social policy (which we believe are in any event usually protected from objective analysis).

MEANINGS OF PROGRAM EVALUATION

Program evaluation has no uniform and consistently applied definition. Instead, the term has become a subject of a variety of interpretations in relation to its purposes, scope, and methodology.

This chapter develops a perspective — and a definition — for program evaluation that is suited to our purpose in this book: that is, to aid those who wish to use evaluation to improve program delivery. We will try to sort out the various issues arising from the bewildering array of current definitions. This should put the reader on a useful course toward understanding the practical significance of program evaluation: How can it serve as a tool for better discharge of program management responsibilities?

We define program evaluation as the *use of scientific methods to measure the implementation and outcomes of programs, for decision-making purposes*. The remainder of this chapter explores this definition.

PROGRAM EVALUATION FOCUSES ON PROGRAM STRUCTURE

In contrast to various other kinds of analysis that might be attempted to examine the quality of program management, evaluation draws attention to the significant "structural" elements of the program — program components, outputs, objectives, and effects. The connections between these elements are vitally important. Let's begin with the program itself.

Program: What Is It?

A *program,* in our practical terms, is an intervention or set of activities mounted to achieve external objectives — that is, to meet some recognized social need or to solve an identified social problem. For example, manpower training programs aim at increasing the employability of their clients while at the same time meeting employers' needs for workers trained in specific skills. Parole services attempt to reduce recidivism — the return of offenders to crime and additional incarceration. Mental health programs may be dedicated to improving the social functioning of mentally handicapped clients. Child welfare programs try to prevent child neglect and to reintegrate weakened or broken families.

Programs are, above all, the embodiment of "ideas" about means of achieving desired social objectives. *How* ideas get implemented and what is their *impact* are the dual concerns of program evaluation, as we see it. How is the program being carried out? Is the program being implemented in the prescribed manner? Is the target population being reached? What are the outcomes of the program? How could the program be more effectively delivered at the client population? These are among the key questions raised by evaluation for the program manager.

Program Components

Typically, programs include several *components*. Program evaluation often cannot provide a global assessment of all these differing services. So we look for the components that would be suitable "units" for evaluation. The rule is that the selected component should be able to be linked to its own external objectives. Here are some examples:

Sheltered workshop program. Components might be (a) supervised employment, (b) counseling, (c) life skills training, and (d) job placement service.

Child protection program. Components might be (a) case work, (b) group work, (c) educational sessions, (d) volunteer services, and (e) drop-in center.

Parole. Components might be (a) individual supervision, (b) groups for alcoholics, (c) family treatment, (d) job placement, and (e) "big brothers" for parolees.

The program manager must distinguish among *program components, operations, and support services.* A component may entail numerous operations. Attention to operations facilitates an understanding of program components. Some examples of operations are: How do we receive clients and arrange for serving them? How do we monitor the clients' receipt of our services? How do we terminate them? Or, in another aspect of program management, how do we direct and control the work of program staff?

Programs are also dependent on internal "support services" — clerical, technical, and professional — and the equipment and procedures that go with them, such as operating and accounting manuals. Are these support elements well organized and managed? How about our financial records and controls? Our budgeting procedures? Our relations with funding authorities? To be sure, these operational and support services are all things with which the program manager must be concerned. But they are not, in our view, the focal issues of program evaluation. To repeat, program evaluation is directed to the program's components — those sets of activities that can be linked to external objectives.

Program Outputs

Program *outputs,* in our terms, are the services delivered by the program. Examples of outputs are: number of individuals served, number of counseling sessions, client contacts or contacts on their behalf (e.g., with other agencies), number of referrals, and number of educational sessions with community groups. The quantification of program outputs makes possible the calculation of workloads and the level of efficiency. Evaluations can examine the extent to which increasing workloads (such as assigning more clients to workers) affects outcomes. For example, how would increasing the size of caseloads for probation officers affect the attainment of the objectives of this program? This kind of analysis can be used to increase the cost-effectiveness of programs.

Program Objectives

Program *objectives* are the formally stated ends to whose achievement the program's resources are directed.[9] Such objectives in social programs are typically mandated by legislatures, Boards of Directors, and often by the funding agency, whatever it may be. Managers are expected to direct resources and program activities toward the achievement of these objectives.

Program objectives are often stated in vague terms — for example, improve social functioning, increase community integration, enhance individual fulfillment. Clarification and practical definition of objectives are essential for both program management and subsequent evaluation. The manager must undertake these tasks if he or she is to provide assurance that measures developed for evaluation reflect the "managerial" understanding of the objectives. Other issues arise with respect to program objectives; we deal with them later, in Chapter 4: Planning the Evaluation.

Program Effects

Effects are, in our view, the unintended consequences of the program's components. Some may be desirable, others may not. Let's take "social assistance" as a program type. Negative (unintended) effects could include such outcomes as "dependency of clients on welfare payments," "disincentives to gainful employment," or one or another stigma experienced by clients ("welfare bums"). The wise program manager uses evaluation to examine these effects in order to find out how pervasive they are and to what extent the program is really responsible for their occurrence. No challenge is greater, we believe, than to manage programs with a degree of subtlety capable of countering their expected but unintended negative effects.

Managers and evaluators should think carefully about the effects as distinct from the formal objectives of their programs.

The aim is not to develop an endless inventory of speculative effects. Rather, the manager should identify those effects that he or she considers sufficiently important to warrant managerial attention. This means that they are also candidates for inclusion in an evaluation.

Linkages: The Glue of Program Structure

Linkages are the connections between the program's components and its outputs, plus the connections between these objectives and those farther out in the hierarchy of intermediate and ultimate objectives. Take, for example, a family counseling component of an urban welfare program. Its output is measured by the number of clients counseled. Its immediate objective is to reduce anxiety. Intermediate objectives might include better family relations, with ultimate objectives of better functioning on the job and improved social relations generally.

Linkages are the expression of the logic of the program structure. Evaluation pays great attention to such cause-and-effect relationships. It discovers and either verifies their validity or denies it. Evaluations oriented toward process or implementation are useful for identifying such possible linkages between program components, outputs, objectives, and effects. Such evaluations thus are used to develop models of the program's structure and underlying logic. Linkages considered plausible can be tested in outcome-oriented evaluations.

PROGRAM EVALUATION IS CONCERNED WITH IMPLEMENTATION AS WELL AS OUTCOMES

Program evaluation does not restrict itself, in our view, to program outcomes. It is also deeply concerned with the implementation processes of the program.

Program implementation studies attempt to describe how the program is being carried out. They help the program manager understand the manner in which program activities are being delivered: The aim is to use the findings to modify program activities to have the best chance of achieving specified objectives. Such studies are useful for subsequent evaluation of effectiveness, inspiring confidence that the evaluation will be focused on program components that are in fact susceptible to being implemented in the prescribed manner.

Attention to program implementation is important as part of effectiveness evaluations. Failure to look at program implementation presents a dilemma. Was the program poorly implemented or was it truly ineffective? Unless the evaluation documents the manner in which the program was implemented, the "goodness of the idea" underlying the program cannot be differentiated from the quality of program administration.

Studies that deal with both program processes and outcomes are also useful because they focus attention on areas for decision by the manager. They permit the manager to draw conclusions about the manner in which the program was implemented (e.g., length, frequency and types of interviews, sessions) and about the outcomes or "results" obtained. In such cases, examination of program processes explains how the program's activities relate (or do not relate) to the outcomes. The manager is then able to use findings to change programs in ways shown to produce the best results.

SCIENTIFIC METHODS: OPTIONS ON RIGOR

When we talk about scientific methods, we refer to objective and systematic methods of conducting an evaluation. But a scientific approach, with a minimum of subjective elements, itself comprises many different levels of rigor.

We cannot define the range of possible options on rigor for each conceivable situation, but the extreme positions are easily explained. At the subjective end of the continuum are evaluations based on intuition and judgment backed up by little or no hard evidence. From day to day in their work, managers are always evaluating their programs in this way. They have their own perceptions. They get feedback from their staff, complaints from their clients, and comments from members of outside monitors or funding agencies. They also have the most detailed knowledge of program finances. They often reflect on the quality of service being received by clients. They come to conclusions and take action to improve the delivery of the program. While we are not suggesting that intuition and judgment should be curtailed, a subjective process of evaluation is not the type we are talking about in this book.

At the scientific end of the evaluation continuum are evaluations carried out with rigorous scientific methods predicated on the achievement of maximum objectivity — in other words, on the achievement of demonstrable and supportable results from the evaluation analysis. This often, but not necessarily, implies a heavy component of quantitative research and inference from "facts." Because of the methodology used, the inferences are assumed to be credible and "actionable." Even within the scientific approaches to evaluation, however, the question of options on rigor remains: How much is enough? Part of the answer comes from the *economics of the evaluation itself.* How much rigor can we afford? What would it mean to the validity of the results? Is some initially suggested plan feasible, or should we look for more economical methods? This is, in short, a cost-benefit question in this respect.

We do not here press for any particular type of scientific methodology. Various kinds of generally accepted approaches are available for the collection of qualitative or quantitative data and for setting up research designs. The manager needs an approach that is tailored to the characteristics of the program. It should be suitable for the purposes of the evaluation. It should take into account the state of the art on research, cost, and whatever political, legal, ethical, and administrative constraints that condition the evaluation effort. At this point, we are simply alerting the program manager to the issue of methodological rigor. It affects the credibility of the evaluation, which in turn affects how far its results can be relied on by the manager to make major decisions on changes in program delivery.

PROGRAM EVALUATION INCLUDES BOTH PERIODIC STUDIES AND ONGOING MONITORING SYSTEMS

Many social program managers think of an evaluation as a study of some kind, done at intervals under suitable terms of reference. In this scenario, the program "waits" for some inde-terminate period — perhaps several years — for the next evalu-ation. In other words, this perception lends itself to periodic, one-shot studies. The mounting disenchantment with program evaluation is at least partly due to the problems associated with periodic evaluations — their cost, their lack of inclusiveness, and their tendency to being not timely for required decisions on either funding priorities or changes in program delivery. Pro-grams have a habit of changing; readers of an evaluation may be perusing a report on a program that no longer exists. The (relevant) modified program has in effect just missed an evalua-tion — which may not be scheduled to recur for some years.

An alternative is to implement ongoing measurement sys-tems that can be integrated with program delivery and normal requirements for administrative records.[10] For example, background information and baseline data on factors the pro-gram aims to change can be collected as part of accepting referrals and doing intake. Data on the services provided to the clients can be collected on an ongoing basis. Measurement of the changes the program aims to effect can be taken at specified times during the treatments, at termination, or during a follow-up period. In other words, the basic data requirements can often be met through an ongoing measurement system. From time to time, a study could be mounted, rolling up the data on hand, supplementing them where necessary with addi-tional data, or complementing the procedure with additional research methods (e.g., setting up a control group).

USE OF PROGRAM EVALUATION FOR
DECISION MAKING

The program manager should expect program evaluation to be a useful tool for decisions on the program. He or she should take steps to ensure that it works out this way. Harry Havens has suggested that useful results can come from even imperfect evaluations, but the rule still holds:

> The utility of the findings, however, is directly related to the
> ability of the evaluator to provide information (however qual-

ified it must be) which is relevant to the decision which must be made.[11]

Once again, we see that the purposes of the evaluation are paramount. What key questions will it answer for the manager? What, if anything, will it provide for external audiences such as the legislature or the Board of Directors? The "activities" of an evaluation all have to be dedicated to a set of managerially defined purposes.

PROGRAM EVALUATION SHOULD NOT BE CONFUSED WITH OTHER MANAGEMENT TOOLS

We referred earlier in this chapter, briefly, to the relatively narrow focus of evaluation per se. We were trying to define, in a simple and useful fashion, what we feel is the proper domain of this managerial initiative. Evaluation is a management tool. But it should not be confused with other analytical techniques and review mechanisms. Program evaluation's distinctive feature is that it is concerned with the *program*. It addresses questions about both the implementation of the program's activities and their resulting outcomes. Other tools of management are typically restricted to management *processes*, rather than with the issues of program delivery and outcome. Let's look at some of the process-oriented concerns of management that lie outside the purview of evaluation.

Even such wide-ranging a function as *planning* is a suitable illustration of this point. Planning entails prospective analysis — e.g., analyzing social problems, determining needs, studying costs and benefits of optional ways of dealing with these needs. Properly carried out, planning considers the findings of program evaluations, but its kind of *front-end analysis* for making long-term decisions should not be confused with the *retrospective findings* of evaluation (what has happened to the program in the past).

Take personnel appraisals as another illustration. These are concerned with the performance of managers and staff. Weakly motivated or incompetent staff can certainly affect the quality of program outcomes. Nevertheless, program evaluation does not provide an adequate base for a fair assessment of employee performance, person by person. We have ample access to appraisal systems without squeezing the function into program evaluation.

Day-to-day management vigilance is expressed in many ways — and it is an important ingredient in good management. Good managers monitor their programs closely. "Paying excruciating attention to detail" is one of the keys to success. The manager looks for wasted time and effort. He or she upgrades weak procedures and documentation. Unauthorized activities, improper expenditures, lost money, and many other details of administration are always being tracked and corrected. The manager carries out studies, from time to time, on ways to make the program more economical and efficient. While these managerial tasks obviously have a bearing on program delivery and effectiveness, they are not the focus of program evaluation.

CONCLUSIONS

We have presented a perspective on program evaluation that serves the interests of managers in improving the delivery of the program rather than an approach oriented toward budgetary decisions by funding agencies. We emphasize the importance of examining program implementation, since this allows the manager to tinker, modify, and make the program more responsive in meeting client needs and more successful in dealing with their problems.

The methodological approach that we present in the remainder of the book is consistent with this basic perspective. Methodology should be selected so as to meet the practical decision-making needs of the manager. It should relate to the characteristics of the program, the cost of doing the evaluation, and the type of information needed for decisions.

NOTES

1. Cited in Sidney E. Zimbolist, *Historic Themes and Landmarks in Social Welfare Research* (New York: Harper & Row, 1977), p. 235.

2. Ibid., p. 247.

3. Richard C. Cabot, "Treatment in Social Case Work and the Need of Criteria and of Tests in Its Success or Failure," *Proceedings of the National Conference of Social Work* (1931): 23-24.

4. Edwin Powers and Helen L. Witmer, *An Experiment on the Prevention of Delinquency – the Cambridge-Somerville Youth Study* (New York: Columbia University Press, 1951).

5. Henry J. Meyer, Edgard F. Borgatta, and Wyatt C. Jones, *Girls at Vocational High* (New York: Russell Sage Foundation, 1965).

6. Gordon E. Brown (ed.) *The Multi-Problem Dilemma* (Metuchen, NJ: Scarecrow Press, 1968).

7. For reference, see Edward T. Mullen, "Evaluation Research on the Effects of Professional Intervention," in Paul C. Vrooman (ed.) *Trans-Disciplinary Issues in Social Welfare* (Waterloo: Wilfrid Laurier University, 1975), p. 25.

8. Harold W. Demone et al., "Evaluation in One Context of Developments in Human Services," in C. Clifford Attkisson and others (eds.) *Evaluation of Human Service Programs* (New York: Academic Press, 1978), p. 34.

9. We are inclined to say that "objectives" and "goals" usually mean the same thing. The literature generally considers objectives to be broad statements of intent and goals to be specific, time-limited targets.

10. See, for example, Daniel Glaser, *Routinizing Evaluation: Getting Feedback on Effectiveness of Crime and Delinquency Programs* (Rockville, MD: National Institute of Mental Health, 1973).

11. Harry S. Havens, "Program Evaluation and Program Management," *Public Administration Review* (July/August 1981): 382.

Chapter 2

PURPOSES OF EVALUATION

In this chapter, we are trying both to provide an overview of the major purposes of evaluation and to emphasize one of them — the *use of evaluation for improving program delivery and making it more responsive to client needs.* However, even a study with better program delivery as its main purpose need not totally ignore, or be unresponsive to, other purposes. Thus a "managerial" evaluation might go part way toward satisfying demands for accountability by external groups. It might also provide useful insights into the nature and impact of specific kinds of social intervention, adding to the society's store of knowledge and contributing to the design or improvement of other programs in the future.

Below, we review these three types of purpose for evaluation: (1) more meaningful accountability, (2) improved program delivery, and (3) addition to the knowledge of the social sciences.[1] We illustrate the types of questions and methodologies that would be suited to each. And we also discuss some of the issues pertinent to each differing purpose. By way of a cautionary comment, we describe briefly some of the hidden, or "covert," purposes for doing evaluations — such as to whitewash a program, to intentionally destroy it, or to avoid (or postpone) action needed on some problem in its management. We begin with evaluation's linkage to accountability.

ACCOUNTABILITY RESULTS FROM RESPONSIBILITY

The demand for accountability (to funding bodies, legislative groups, and to some extent the public) has been the major impetus for program evaluation in the past few years. Fiscal constraints have increased the competition of public agencies for available dollars and raised questions of "value for money" from their activities. The "accountability perspective" on evaluation holds that the worth of the program must be reported and thereby demonstrated if it is to deserve continued legislative, financial, and public support. Note that this is a restricted view of accountability, even at that. It ignores the internal dimensions of bureaucratic accountability in day-to-day program management. From the outsider's perspective, however, relevant questions are: Is the program being implemented as it was originally authorized and funded? Is it achieving its objectives? Are the clients and public satisfied with the program? How does the program compare with other alternative means of pursuing the same objectives? Is the program achieving its objectives in the most efficient manner? What are its unintended effects — particularly negative ones?

The use of program evaluation as a tool or medium of accountability is reflected in numerous historical developments. At the federal level in the United States, for example, the Congressional Budget and Impoundment Control Act of 1974 provides for program analysis, appraisal, and evaluation. Title VII of the Act authorizes congressional committees to carry out evaluation studies, to contract for such studies, or to require government agencies to perform them. It also requires the General Accounting Office, as an agency of the Congress — "the watchdog of Washington" — to review and evaluate the administration's programs. A mandate for legislative auditors to examine the evaluation activities of government departments has also been given to the Auditor General of Canada, as well as to several of his provincial counterparts in that country.

Legislative and funding bodies have on occasion made the establishment and financing of programs contingent on evaluation being carried out at specified intervals. In the United States, this has taken the form of setting aside funds for program evaluation. For example, in 1975 the new legislation for community mental health centers (Public Law 94-63, Section 206) required centers to set aside 2 percent of their annual operating expenditures for "continuing evaluation of the effectiveness of its programs . . . and . . . for a review of the quality of the services provided by the center."

Recent years have also witnessed a growing interest in so-called sunset legislation. Programs are established initially for a specified number of years — giving them, in effect, a legislated day on which their sun will predictably set. Every, say, five years such programs have to be evaluated and reauthorized. Otherwise, they die. The relevance to program evaluations is that the findings from them are expected to contribute to policy determination when the program is up for reauthorization. Even though sunset legislation has not been adopted widely across the U.S. civil service, a number of programs are being funded with built-in sunset clauses. We may see more and more sunset-type evaluations. After all is said and done, it is relatively easy for legislatures to insert statutory duration into enabling legislation; it tends to enhance their future power over shifts in public policy.

Program evaluation is also expected to add to accountability within the budgetary or resource-allocation process. It is included, for example, as a major element in planning programming and budgeting (PPB). Partly because program effectiveness data have not improved noticeably in either coverage or quality, much of the enthusiasm has gone out of the PPB movement.[2]

Similarly, program evaluation has, as might be expected, been linked to the budgeting process in current efforts to apply zero base budgeting. This linkage has been recognized by the Office of Management and Budget in Washington: "By encouraging agencies to build on the performance measures used for Zero Base Budgeting, we hope we can tie the program evaluation efforts more closely to the all-important budget process."[3]

Numerous reasons help explain this important linkage between program evaluation and accountability. The public is obviously concerned about the levels of government expenditure in the United States and Canada, as well as in other countries. Taxpayer revolts are one manifestation. Public concern over the inflationary impact of federal deficits is another. Budgetary restraint has attained a high priority. Thus program evaluation comes to be viewed as a responsible means of arriving at difficult decisions on the reallocation of resources. We are also witnessing negative attitudes toward many government programs — especially social programs whose objectives are often difficult to specify and hard to rationalize in express terms. The conservative trend is strengthened by accumulating evidence from evaluations showing disappointing results from many social programs.

MANAGEMENT CONCERN IS WITH PROGRAM IMPROVEMENT

The management perspective on program evaluation sees it as a tool for making improved decisions about the design of programs and their delivery and about the type and amount of resources that should be devoted to the program. In this case, the line manager is the client of the evaluation study. He or she views it as a source of improved *management control,* that is, as a source of information for managerial action.

Program evaluation can address several information needs of line managers: How is the program being implemented? Is it being carried out in the prescribed manner? What is the nature of the impediments to the implementation of the program? What appear to be the outcomes or consequences of the program? Are the objectives being achieved? To what extent does the program produce unintended effects? How does the manner in which the program is being implemented affect its outcomes? What types of factors impede or facilitate the achievement of its objectives? What types of clients appear to gain the most benefit from the program? Is a new type of service or a different way of deliverying an existing service worth introducing as a pilot experiment? On a large scale?

The major rationale for program evaluation in this context is that responsible management requires the types of information it can produce. Program managers simply *must* understand how their program is being implemented and how the specifics of their operation affect its outcomes. The primary use of information here is to modify services and delivery mechanisms in order to increase their effectiveness. The key question raised by the previously mentioned accountability perspective was: "Is the program any good?" The central question from the management perspective is: "How can the program be made better?" In other words, while program evaluation from the accountability perspective is used for making major policy or resource allocation decisions, from the management perspective it is employed primarily to generate improvements to the program.

However, as we indicated earlier, evaluations that are primarily meant to serve program management can also be useful for accountability purposes. Answers to the questions in the preceding paragraph are also somewhat relevant to the accountability question. But the main emphasis is on improved program delivery.

KNOWLEDGE: ACADEMIC ENRICHMENT

Program evaluation can also be used to produce knowledge that may or may not be of immediate use to decision makers (either program managers or the people to whom they are accountable). It contributes, in this perspective, to potentially important additions to the state of the art in different fields of practice. Such research may indeed be devoid of practical impact in the immediate future. On the other hand, it may lay the foundations for far-reaching program innovations in the longer term. We must keep in mind the tradition of academic inquiry in assessing social conditions and interventions designed to affect them. Producing knowledge for the field is, therefore, one of the functions of program evaluation.

Examples abound of evaluations carried out by professionals or private foundations where the primary purpose is to develop knowledge about particular interventions and the theories underlying them. For example, the Vera Institute of Justice has carried out numerous evaluations in the field of criminal justice. These include studies of the impact that the installation of telephones in detention facilities would have on the likelihood of people making arrangements to be released;[4] and the impact of allowing poor people who are unable to post bail to be released on their own recognizance.[5] The Police Foundation has carried out several evaluations of such demonstration projects as preventative patrol and team policing. George Fairweather spent more than twenty years conducting research on the problems of mental patients released from hospitals, examining the effectiveness of interventions that existed at the time and developing and testing new interventions in terms of their effectiveness.[6] These types of studies are not usually carried out by people or organizations directly involved in program funding or management, but by those curious about the impact of social programs. Their aim is to produce knowledge for the field, as opposed to meeting the specific information needs of managers, monitors, or governors.

The common use of demonstration projects and experiments also fits into the knowledge perspective. Various types of innovative services are funded for the purpose of testing their effectiveness. The rationale for funding the services is to evaluate them. Findings may lead to eventual changes in public policy. For example, the Manhattan Bail Bond experiment showed that accused people could be successfully released prior to trial without bail. The idea of bail-free release was extended to federal defendents and written into the Bail Reform Act of 1966. Admittedly, such dramatic use of this kind of evaluation research has been rare.[7]

COVERT PURPOSES

Finally, a word of caution on the dangers of hidden, or "covert," purposes for the evaluation.[8] Evaluations may be undertaken to whitewash a program — to make it look good. The type of methodology that can accomplish this end is therefore invoked (e.g., asking questions about client satisfaction with services). Another covert purpose may be to destroy the program. Again, evaluations can be used to avoid action or postpone it where a more honest, objective review would point clearly to needed changes (e.g., in the nature of the services, the level of funding, number and quality of staff, location and kind of facilities). The evaluation might also be carried out as a token response to some requirement and have little if any practical significance of any kind.

Covert purposes, or the possibility of their lurking within the evaluation process, is one reason why program managers are understandably nervous about the accountability demands of evaluation sponsors. They worry about the use of evaluation for answering life-and-death questions of program survival. They are also concerned that a program may be held accountable for the unrealistic goals specified at its birth but which are no longer ones for which it should, realistically, be held accountable now. Moreover, managers worry about the use of inconclusive findings for the making of major decisions on public policy. Yet the impression of scientific objectivity that may come from massive numerical compilations can be misused in the reaching of subsequent funding decisions. The fact is that evaluations rarely produce definitive results. Qualifications are almost invariably attached to the findings. But they can be all too easily overlooked by authorities who feel obliged to act.

CONCLUSIONS

These three differing perspectives of program evaluation — accountability, management, and scientific curiosity — are not all mutually exclusive. A study done from the management

Exhibit 2.1   Key Features of the Accountability and Managerial
               Perspectives in Program Evaluation

	Accountability Perspective	Managerial Perspective
Client	External authority	Program manager
Focus	Ultimate objectives	Processes and immediate/ intermediate objectives
Purpose	Decision on fate of program	Improvement of program delivery and impact
Methodology	Scientifically objective	Enough rigor to support sound decisions
Data	Largely quantitative	Qualitative and quantitative

perspective can at the same time meet at least some of the
requirements of accountability. It may have by-products for the
knowledge base of various disciplines. However, a primary
commitment to one perspective as opposed to another is likely
to have major consequences for the organizational arrangements for program evaluation and for the design and execution
of evaluation studies.

We can point out the implications of having evaluations that
focus on a particular perspective by comparing what would
occur if an evaluator attempted to satisfy the accountability
versus the management perspective. The outline in Exhibit
2.1 presents the two perspectives and a capsulized summary
of the key features of each type of evaluation.

Clearly, the perspective makes the difference. In any kind of
evaluation, intellectual honesty and de facto objectivity are of
fundamental importance. The problem has been well stated in
Miles' Law: "Where you stand depends on where you sit."[9]
One can scarcely expect managerially oriented evaluators to
recommend organizational suicide to a program manager.
Hence decisions on the fate of programs are not likely to come
from internal evaluations. On the other hand, the manager

needs the best and most objective evaluation data for engineering changes in program delivery. In both cases, methodology has to suit the purposes.

Our own feeling is that accountability-related evaluations will continue to have problems of acceptability for both scientific and political reasons. They will continue to be carried out and will always have a place in the scheme of things, but, in our view, the management-oriented evaluation has yet to come into its own. We believe that it offers new tools for better program delivery and deserves the careful attention of every program manager.

NOTES

1. This typology is found in Eleanor Chelimsky, "Differing Perspectives of Evaluation," *New Directions for Program Evaluation* 2 (Summer 1978): 1-18.

2. Carol Weiss, *Evaluation Research* (Englewood Cliffs, NJ: Prentice-Hall, 1972), p. 90; see also Allen Schick, "A Death in the Bureaucracy: The Demise of Federal PPB," *Public Administration Review* (March/April 1973): 146-156.

3. *Hearings Before the Committee on Human Resources,* 95th Cong., October 6 and 27, 1977 (Washington, DC: Government Printing Office, 1978), p. 5.

4. Kenneth J. Lenihan, "Telephones and Raising Bail: Some Lessons in Evaluation," *Evaluation Quarterly* 2, 4 (November 1977): 569-586.

5. B. Botein, "The Manhattan Bail Project," *Texas Law Review* 43 (1965): 319-331.

6. George W. Fairweather, David H. Sanders, and Louis G. Tornatzky, *Creating Change in Mental Health Organizations* (Elmsford: Pergamon Press, 1975).

7. A view shared by Harry Havens: "One hopes the results are a useful contribution to basic research, but there is not much evidence of this either." See his "Program Evaluation and Program Management," *Public Administration Review* (July/August 1981): 481.

8. For further discussion, see Edward Suchman, *Evaluation Research* (New York: Russell Sage Foundation, 1967).

9. Rufus E. Miles, Jr., "The Origin and Meaning of Miles' Law," *Public Administration Review* (September/October 1978): 399-403.

Chapter 3

STEPS IN THE EVALUATION PROCESS

The evaluation process begins with a number of broad preparatory steps that set the stage for more specific ones related to management of the evaluation project. The manager works his or her way through these before getting down to details of the evaluation effort:

- Make a formal commitment to the idea of doing one or more evaluations.
- Communicate this policy to program staff.
- Form an initial judgment on scale and budget.
- Decide on professional leadership.
- Define the roles of all the parties to an evaluation exercise.

Once the manager has established these underlying conditions for the evaluation, these specific steps follow:

- Make up a program component profile.
- Select program components for evaluation.
- Plan the evaluation through the evaluability assessment.
- Decide on who will do the evaluation research.
- Draw up an agreement between the manager and the evaluator.

- Implement the evaluation and monitor its progress.
- Report results and develop action plans.

The material dealing with these matters is the core of this book. Subsequent chapters elaborate on evaluation activities related to executing the various steps. Chapter 4 deals in more detail with evaluability assessment. Chapter 5 discusses how to acquire needed information. Chapter 6 describes the manager's role in choice of an effective design for the evaluation. Finally, Chapter 7 provides guidelines on how the manager can use the results of the evaluation to improve program delivery.

SET THE STAGE

Setting the stage for program evaluation is essential: It establishes the preconditions for planning and carrying out the work in a manner most likely to yield practical information for managerial decisions.

MAKE A FORMAL COMMITMENT TO PROGRAM EVALUATION

The manager must be committed to program evaluation in order to ensure the involvement and cooperation of program staff, the relevance of the exercise, and the use of findings for making program changes. This commitment can be expressed in various ways. The manager can identify him- or herself as the primary client for program evaluation and enunciate the purposes it is expected to serve. The establishment of a senior advisory group to be involved in planning the evaluations and interpreting their findings is another way of reflecting managerial commitment. Establishing formal links between evaluations and the planning functions of the organization further consolidates the manager's commitment to this kind of effort.

COMMUNICATE THE POLICY TO PROGRAM STAFF

The manager should communicate his or her commitment to the program staff. The evaluation aim should be made clear in this initial orientation. Care is needed: The evaluation(s) should not be advertised under false labels such as personnel evaluation, organization study, or as part of the employee appraisal process, and so on.

The orientation phase gives the manager an opportunity to generate understanding and commitment by all his or her employees. It also provides a place to start on recognizing their inputs to the work, among other things explaining possible disruptions to program delivery that may be foreseen as likely to be created by the evaluation.

FORM AN INITIAL JUDGMENT ON SCALE AND BUDGET

Before detailed plans are made for use of specific evaluation methods, the manager should have in mind the amount of time and money that he or she feels would be justified for doing the research. This "scale" of evaluation effort may, of course, change somewhat when the planning for a specific effort gets under way. But the manager should announce the probable budgetary constraints right at the start. This may sound difficult. In practice it is not. Program managers are usually well aware of the limits of program management change likely to come from several different kinds of evaluation. This means that they have a quite sound appreciation of the basic economics of evaluation in cost-benefit terms.

DECIDE ON PROFESSIONAL LEADERSHIP

In light of announced purposes and the general scale of evaluation effort envisaged, the manager then decides on the kind of professional leadership needed for the study. Will an evaluation group be set up, without program responsibilities, to take the lead? Will an evaluation be directed by a program staff member? With outside professional help from consultants? Or will it be best to employ an external evaluator to spearhead the project? How will internal program staff support be arranged?

The resolution of questions pertaining to project leadership and support depends on many considerations. First, the size of the program and the proposed scope of evaluation activities help determine whether or not a separate evaluation group and external expertise can be afforded. Second, the availability of evaluation specialists on staff or the use of competent program officers needs to be taken into account. Third, the avoidance of "bias" is a concern that affects many decisions on these matters. We believe that some element of bias occurs in all evaluations, no matter how they are conducted or who does them. The manager needs to assess the bias associated with differing options and make leadership decisions that take account of this factor. Fourth, the manager has to consider the balance between use of program staff and outsiders — the former with greater familiarity with the program and the latter with perhaps more expertise or more objectivity. What is the best mix?

DEFINE THE ROLES OF THE PARTIES

Once the evaluation team's composition has been settled, the manager defines the roles of the various parties to the research: his or her own role and those of the advisory committee, director of the evaluation, evaluation staff, program staff, and clients. This step clarifies the nature of the evaluation process. It may also provide for "expert review" of plans, draft reports, and the final report, as well as for the distribution of the final report.

Once these initial phases are completed, the stage is set for the steps in the evaluation process itself.

MAKE UP A PROGRAM COMPONENT PROFILE

The first substantive step in the evaluation process is the preparation of a *profile of the program's components*. This is typically an in-house job. It sets out what program people (and their enabling authority) see as the activities constituting the components of the program and their outputs, objectives and effects. Exhibit 3.1 provides a format for preparation of a program component profile.

The profile enables the manager to reexamine the structure and logic of the program. He or she asks: Do we know what we are trying to do in this program? Are the objectives clear? Inclusive? Are some of our objectives outworn? How plausible is the rationale linking program components, outputs and objectives/effects? Should additional objectives and effects be included? In short, the component profile allows the manager to formulate hypotheses about the strengths and weaknesses of program design, as reflected in current delivery problems. This is a valuable exercise. It is likely to have a number of unexpected immediate benefits for program management. Most important for evaluation, it permits organizing the evaluation of key program components likely to benefit from it.

PLAN THE EVALUATION THROUGH EVALUABILITY ASSESSMENT

Evaluability assessment is the front-end analysis that enables the manager to decide the extent to which the program can appropriately and reasonably be evaluated. This is a critically important step. We deal with it at some length later, in Chapter 4. "Appropriately" means that a suitable methodology can be found to answer the questions on implementation and impact that the manager has formulated. Otherwise, he or she is stuck. "Reasonably" means that the subsequent evaluation's results will be worth what they cost. Evaluability assessment needs more attention as a prelude to decisions on the design of evaluations.[1]

The evaluability assessment analyzes the nature of the program, its activities, and its delivery mechanisms — and clarifies its objectives and effects in relation to what is being done to cause them. It assesses the feasibility of applying any desired evaluation research methodology — which may indicate changes in the evaluation budget. At this step in the process, the manager ensures that the best terms of reference for the projected evaluation are compiled: focus, information to be collected, research design required, how much manpower and

PROGRAM COMPONENT

PROFILE

PROGRAM: _____

_____

COMPONENT: _____

_____

BUDGET: _____ PERSON-YEARS: _____

DIRECTOR/SUPERVISOR: _____

DESCRIPTION OF COMPONENT (ACTIVITIES/SERVICES): _____

_____

_____

_____

_____

OUTPUTS: _____

_____

_____

_____

OBJECTIVES: _____

_____

_____

_____

Exhibit 3.1   *(continued)*

EFFECTS: _____

_____

_____

_____

Exhibit 3.1 Continued

money will be needed to do the work, and the time required to carry it out.

Note that evaluability is a matter of degree. The main concern of evaluability assessment is to determine the extent to which a program can be evaluated, not to make a yes or no decision on the matter. A relative judgment is made about whether the purposes of the evaluation can be achieved, considering such factors as the current state of the art in evaluation research, the methodological requirements of the proposed study, its probable cost, and the constraints affecting the conduct of the evaluation.

DECIDE ON WHO WILL DO THE STUDY

Once the policy decision has been made to carry out an evaluation, the program component(s) selected, and the evaluability assessment completed, the manager then has to decide just who is going to do this study. He or she already has given some thought to this matter during the preliminary phases of setting the stage for the undertaking. At this point, however, the final decisions are made. We have already discussed the question of study leadership, when the basic staffing philosophy of the project was settled. A number of considerations should now guide the manager in selecting the individual members of the evaluation team.

EXPERIENCE IN PROGRAM EVALUATION

Key members of the evaluation team should have had relevant past experience in program evaluation, preferably under conditions resembling those of this particular situation. People from evaluation projects in other similar agencies are a possibility. So are outside consultants who may have specialized in certain aspects of the subject pertinent to this effort.

RANGE OF METHODOLOGICAL COMPETENCE

Evaluating social programs presents both challenges and opportunities for research methodology. Competence in this area is a must. The manager looks for people who are not wedded to one particular prevailing methodology and who can put up exciting alternatives within the qualitative and quantitative paradigms. The manager, in other words, looks for creative talent and ingenuity as well as experience. This is important. It can have a dramatic impact on evaluation costs as well as on the credibility of results.

ABILITY TO RELATE TO MANAGEMENT

The manager is looking for advice on how to improve the implementation and impact of his or her program. The evaluation team has to be able to respond. Its members, or most of them, at least, should be able to relate to the information needs of management. This will support the usefulness of the results. More specifically, the manager looks for this element so that he or she will not be presented with "blue sky" ideas beyond the range of practical application or — worse that this — reflections and conclusions that lack an actionable basis of any kind.

BALANCE OF TECHNICAL AND ADMINISTRATIVE SKILLS

The manager looks for an evaluation team with both technical and administrative skills. Technical competence underwrites the credibility of results. Administrative know-how means that the evaluation will in fact be carried out in a timely and efficient fashion. The project should be directed, operationally, by a competent administrator — ideally one who also understands the program being evaluated and its internal politics, personalities, and environmental problems.

DRAW UP AGREEMENT BETWEEN
MANAGER AND EVALUATOR

The manager and the evaluation team, or specifically its director, must have a practical working agreement on what is to be done and how.[2] This clarifies the critical issues of study requirements and the respective responsibilities of manager and evaluator. Objective: To identify issues in advance and forestall misunderstandings or enable those that arise to be dealt with more readily. An agreement could cover items such as:

- *breakdown of expenditures* for the evaluation
- *scope of the evaluation* – e.g., the number of sites, clients, and types of services covered
- evaluation *project schedule* and milestone reporting dates for project control
- specification of the *research design* and *data collection procedures*
- *responsibilities of program staff* in carrying out evaluation tasks or in their work on the program itself
- *management commitment regarding program delivery* during the period when the evaluation is being carried out
- *controls to ensure adherence to the evaluation plan* (e.g., means of checking whether random assignment procedures were properly followed or if staff are keeping proper records)
- the *consultative process* to be followed, including the preparation of progress reports and the nature of feedback sessions with relevant groups
- *publicity on the project* and on release of findings

IMPLEMENT THE EVALUATION
AND MONITOR ITS PROGRESS

The "action" step is doing the evaluation in a way that allows the manager to monitor and control its progress. Timetable and interim reporting dates, meetings, reviews, and so on are central to this step. So is a procedure for controlling the flow of funds. It goes without saying that every monitoring process is tailored to its particular circumstance. The more uncertain the manager is about the ability of colleagues and consultants to execute their plan in a timely fashion and within budget, the more detailed is the approach to managerial monitoring and control. "Paying attention to details" in evaluation exercises is just as important as it is in every other aspect of program management.

Technical matters also come up for their share of the manager's attention. Provision should be made for monitoring the research techniques being employed in the evaluation: sampling, randomization procedures, completion of questionnaires, and the like.

During the evaluation, the manager will likely discover several factors tending to deflect the work from its original purpose, its established research design, or its methods of data collection. For example, early investigation may suggest that problems in curriculum content are emerging as much more important than weaknesses in instructional methods, or that one of the components being evaluated has much more severe problems than another. The design of the evaluation may have to be modified. Its data collection procedures, for example, as they embody the use of self-administered questionnaires, may turn out to be ineffectual and call for a microsample based on personal interviews with respondents. The timetable of the evaluation may be put under pressure from such events. The manager should be ready to change directions and schedules and make the decisions needed to keep the project on a successful path.

ANALYZE RESULTS AND DEVELOP ACTION PLANS

Throughout the planning and execution phases of the evaluation, the manager has had his or her sights fixed firmly on the final report — planned to be suitable for its various internal and external audiences. The final report is a key document. The evaluation plan provides for it to be properly designed, drafted, and possibly subjected to an expert review prior to submission to the program manager. The manager then disseminates the report to its intended receivers.

One way of ensuring that the manager is suitably informed about the parameters of study interpretation is for him or her to insist that the report be presented in understandable language — the criterion here is the "intelligent but uninformed reader." Evaluation reports should have plainly stated explanations of their data analysis, no matter how esoteric the technology on which they are based. The manager must insist on this, where necessary, to flush out the sensitive areas between objective analysis and technicians' interpretation of findings. *Reports should be preceded by detailed plans of their contents and conclusions for the prior review of the program manager.* In this connection, submission of draft reports to the program manager is definitely *not* the first step — at that stage reports are so near completion that the manager cannot cope with them or induce modifications. The outline stage is when this must be done, and the manager should insist on it.

Given the final report and its dissemination, the manager has then to consider planning to take actions based on it. Under our scheme of things, it has been planned with this thought in mind. Using the results of evaluations typically involves a series of identifiable steps (see Chapter 7).

The first step is to set the priorities for decisions and actions based on the outcomes of the study. A group of people to act as advisors or a "sounding board" for the manager is usually helpful at this stage.

When *what* has to be done has been decided, the manager prepares a timetable that reflects the settled priorities. He or she establishes improvement projects to deal with each aspect of the implementation plan, with suitable resources and controls. This step, then, means deciding *how* the program changes are going to be effected.

Based on these decisions, the manager launches the improvement projects and monitors and controls them — making any necessary adjustments en route — to achieve the desired goals of improved program delivery. This experience is then fed back into further actions, including possible future reevaluations to confirm the success of the initial changes.

CONCLUSIONS

Managers who follow the steps we have outlined for the evaluation process should benefit from greatly improved evaluation results. The key to success is to have an evaluation designed to provide the answers to very specific questions about program implementation and impact. These questions should be "practical" ones, formulated to lay the foundation for decisions on program changes. The goal: effective program evaluation. Ensuring the fruitfulness of evaluations is the responsibility of the line manager, shared with but not handed over to, the evaluation team.

NOTES

1. See Leonard Rutman, *Planning Useful Evaluations: Evaluability Assessment* (Beverly Hills, CA: Sage Publications, 1980).

2. For further information, see George W. Fairweather and Louis Tornatzky, *Experimental Methods for Social Policy Research* (New York: Pergamon Press, 1979), pp. 132-137. See also Rutman, *Planning Useful Evaluations*, pp. 187-188.

Chapter 4

PLANNING THE EVALUATION
Evaluability Assessment

This chapter begins with the assumption that the manager has identified a program to be evaluated. Initial decisions have been made on the scale of the research permitted by budgetary conditions. The next step is to carry out an assessment of the "evaluability" of the program. This evaluability assessment explores and determines the "preconditions" needed for an evaluation that will attain its purposes. It indicates the type of evaluation that could appropriately and reasonably be carried out. The manager needs this information before committing resources to any serious evaluation effort. In short, the evaluability assessment establishes the probability of a subsequent evaluation being successful.

The tasks described in this chapter should be carried out by an evaluator, not by the program manager. The program manager's views about the program are part of the input to the assessment, along with those of other people — and someone other than the manager is needed to pull it all together and to recommend to the manager the kind and extent of evaluation that should be seriously considered.

EVALUABILITY ASSESSMENT AIMS AT
CREDIBLE, USEFUL EVALUATIONS

Evaluability assessments aim to ensure *credible* and *useful* evaluations for the program manager. That is their primary purpose. Many shortcomings of evaluations conducted to date could have been avoided had sufficient attention been paid to this important preevaluation work. Its key question: To what extent could the purposes of the intended evaluation be met, considering such factors as the program's characteristics, the available research methodology, cost, and constraints on the use of the desired research methods?

Carol Weiss has emphasized why we should pay attention to program design and implementation in planning an evaluation study:

> The sins of the program are often visited on the evaluation. When programs are well-conceptualized and developed, with clearly defined goals and consistent methods of work, the lot of evaluation is relatively easy. But when programs are disorganized, beset with disruptions, ineffectively designed, or poorly managed, the evaluation falls heir to the problems of the setting.[1]

Many program labels are vague. They may comprehend a variety of different approaches, conveying no coherent message as to the nature of the program. At very least, we must have a proper description of the program so that the type of intervention supposedly being implemented (and assessed) is known in advance. Otherwise, we end up with a "black box" evaluation that draws conclusions about some undefined intervention (such as whether or not casework is effective). From such studies, evaluation findings cannot be meaningfully related to a particular form of intervention — so that it might be encouraged and replicated if the evaluation were positive, or modified and possibly stopped if the evaluation were negative.

Even complex interventions can yield to efforts at definition. For the evaluation conducted by Sloane and colleagues, for example, the interventions were described in several different dimensions for a study of the effectiveness of behavior therapy and psychotherapy: the formal characteristics of the patient-therapist interaction in both situations, the nature of the patient-therapist relationship, and the specific clinical techniques used in treatment.[2]

Evaluability assessment is also used to describe how the program is being implemented as a prelude to decisions on the details of the intended evaluation. If the purpose of the planned evaluation is to determine what particular type of program component is effective, for example, the manager must be assured that the program will continue to be implemented in a "representative" way. This must be conveyed to the evaluator; otherwise, the evaluator may wind up studying something other than what was supposed to be studied. A considerable body of literature has grown up about the failures of program implementation — that is, programs not being put into place according to the intent of the program designers.[3] Failure to recognize problems of program implementation may result in an evaluation that tests the effectiveness of the program but cannot draw a distinction between its poor administration or apparent lack of effectiveness. The evaluability assessment can point out some of these problems of program design and delivery, leading to a possible decision that program evaluation should be focused on understanding program implementation issues rather than on measuring program effectiveness.

In many studies, vague program objectives are assessed without any assurance that the chosen measures are valid for what the program is trying to achieve. We are all aware of the types of objectives that are vague or nebulous — for example, "improve the quality of life," "strengthen leadership resources," "fulfill individual capacities," or "enhance social functioning." Vague objectives are typically the consensus of promotional factions in the discussions leading up to the establishment of new programs. Moreover, vague objectives are popular with some program managers; such objectives provide them with flexibility for changing program activities as future circumstances suggest. On top of this, programs cannot be held accountable in specific terms for nonspecified objectives open to wide interpretation.

When it comes to program evaluation, the result of having vague objectives may be that the evaluator winds up defining them through the selection of measures for the study. This is risky: The evaluation may not be measuring the attainment of the goals toward which the manager feels he or she is working. We have emphasized the importance of specific goals for the completion of successful evaluations. However, the problem is a deeper one. How could anyone *manage* a program in the absence of clarified goals? A program manager would be very short of criteria for mobilizing and directing program resources under such circumstances.

We have also seen numerous examples of evaluations that measure program effectiveness against the obviously unrealistic or overly ambitious initial objectives that were enunciated to support the launching of the program (and for general public consumption) — but not to serve as criteria for later accountability. For example, group counseling by prison guards may influence inmate behavior in a penitentiary, but it is not likely to affect future crime and reincarceration. A manpower training program may increase the employability of individuals who are trained in it, but it cannot be expected to reduce the unemployment rate because the causes of unemployment are not primarily a lack of training but, rather, more general political and economic conditions. Evaluations that attempt to determine the effectiveness of programs whose goals are not realistic predictably produce negative results. Many of the disappointing findings about the effectiveness of social interventions could be traced back to this problem — that is, the evaluation of the attainment of goals that were really meant to gain support for the program but were used instead to hold it accountable in actual operation.

Analysis of the above-mentioned issues of program design and delivery can lead to decisions about the major thrust of subsequent, realistic evaluations — in collecting data to gain an understanding of program delivery and to permit justifiable program modifications. In short, evaluability assessment can often be as useful as the subsequent evaluation in providing directions for change to the manager. Attention paid to these issues can also enhance the manageability of a program, by spotlighting areas for managerial action:

- *poorly defined programs* that require elaboration to facilitate their implementation in the field
- *failure* of management *to implement programs in the prescribed manner*
- *vague objectives* that provide little basis for accountability and insufficient direction for the program manager
- *unrealistic objectives* that are beyond the reach of the program and for which its manager should not be held accountable
- *unintended effects,* negative or positive, that the program is likely to produce
- *varying perceptions* among managers and program staff *about the meaning and priority of objectives*
- *competing or conflicting objectives*

Once the program design and implementation issues have been examined, attention needs to be paid to the feasibility of the type of evaluation that would achieve the desired results. Many of the pitfalls in evaluation can be identified in the preevaluation stage. This helps prevent the needless waste of resources in carrying out evaluations that have little chance of meeting managers' information needs.

The starting point for determining feasibility is to establish the manager's purpose(s) for doing the evaluation. This provides the basis for identifying the methodology required. The evaluability assessment attempts to establish the extent to which the methodological requirements can be applied within the available budget and in view of constraints such as those of a political, legal, ethical, or administrative nature.

STEPS IN ASSESSING THE EVALUABILITY
OF PROGRAMS

In this section, we present a step-by-step guide to evaluators for carrying out an evaluability assessment.[4]

STEP 1: PREPARE A DOCUMENTS MODEL
OF THE PROGRAM

The evaluator begins by preparing a description of the program (components) as it is supposed to be according to available "documents": for example, legislation, funding proposals, published brochures, annual reports, minutes of policymaking groups, administrative manuals. Program documents reflect the formal commitments made through the program — to legislators who voted the money, to clients being served, and to the public. The documents model is the first step for the evaluator in understanding the purposes of the program, its components and outputs, and how these are all (ostensibly) connected. It also serves as the basis for interviews of program staff, by the evaluator, to obtain their views and perceptions about the basic nature of the program.

The process of developing the Documents Model begins with the evaluator listing all program components, outputs, objectives, and effects. The reader should be reminded of the definitions that we provided in Chapter 1.

Once the evaluator has identified all the elements that make up the Documents Model, he or she is in a position to construct this model. In Exhibit 4.1 we present an example of such a model for an employment training program. It has three components:

(a) *On-the-job training:* providing employers with wage reimbursement for providing training to employees covered by the program.

(b) *Training courses:* classroom instruction for helping the program's clients develop basic skills.

(c) *Training allowance:* basic support payments to enrollees, plus reimbursement for expenses incurred while taking training.

We have also identified the relevant outputs for each program component. For example, the output of the training courses is the number of persons trained. Finally, we present the hierarchy of objectives and effects. The logic of the diagram

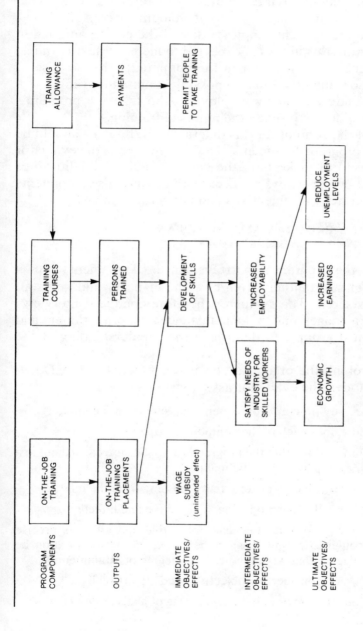

Source: *Audit Guide: Auditing of Procedures for Effectiveness,*
        (Ottawa: Office of the Auditor General of Canada, 1981), p. 14.

Figure 4.1   Documents Model of an Employment Training Program

is that if you achieve the immediate objective, it contributes to the achievement of intermediate and ultimate objectives. Therefore, in our example, the development of skills is expected to increase the employability of the people enrolled in the program; this in turn is expected to increase their earnings and reduce unemployment in the community. In the case of on-the-job training, we have a possible (unintended) effect — a wage subsidy earned by employers who take the program's money but do not provide the requisite training.

All of the content for this diagram in Exhibit 4.1 should be found in program documents. The only inference the evaluator is supposed to make is in the cause-and-effect relationships indicated by the arrows connecting the program's components to the hierarchy of objectives and effects.

INTERVIEW PROGRAM MANAGERS AND DEVELOP A MANAGER'S MODEL

How the program is portrayed in the Documents Model may differ substantially from how the manager and key staff members see it. The evaluator therefore conducts interviews with the manager, and in some instances the practitioners and key interest groups, to determine their understanding of the program.

In probing the organization for refinements to the Documents Model, the evaluator asks questions like these:

(a) Are any program components missing from the model?

(b) How does each of the components operate?

(c) Do you think that the program's activities are carried out in a uniform and systematic manner?

(d) Are any objectives (or effects) missing from the model?

(e) What is the meaning of each objective and effect?

(f) Do you consider that each objective and effect is precise enough to permit measurement (i.e., could information be collected that would indicate its degree of attainment)?

(g) Do you consider the objectives and effects realistic?

(h) Does the program have conflicting objectives and effects?

Manager's models could be developed for each person interviewed. Such an approach would set out, in the perspective of each manager or program supervisor interviewed. Included would be components considered to be well defined and objectives and effects that are specific and realistic. The interview results, in the form of the Manager's Model, should be sent to each respondent for final comment — to ensure that it represents fairly the views of each.

The evaluator then reconciles the differences between the Documents Model and a consolidated Manager's Model. This may shed new light on the degrees of difference between the formal objectives and activities and the operationally defined objectives and activities as perceived by program staff. The differences help the evaluator design the field work that provides direct observational confirmation (or not) of the Manager's Model.

GO INTO THE FIELD TO FIND OUT
WHAT IS REALLY HAPPENING

For most social programs, evaluators have to do field work, to find out what is actually going on in the program — as a prelude to helping the manager decide how it should be evaluated. The Documents Model and the Manager's Model are not usually enough to yield a real understanding of the program's complex activities and the types of impact they may be producing. Field work on the program's activities and processes is also useful for verifying the Program Model as developed as a result of this work (see next section). The evaluator is particularly sensitive to possible unintended effects not mentioned thus far by the people interviewed in the program.

Through the field work, the evaluator tries to understand, in detail, the manner in which the program is being implemented. He or she compares actual operations with published guidelines to the staff — performance versus prescription. In particular, where the managers have had trouble explaining the nature of their interventions, the evaluator can check to see if, in fact, a systematic intervention of *any* kind is being effected.

The evaluator can also try to find out just what groups are being served by the program, especially in relation to any target population. He or she also collects information on the nature and seriousness of client's problems. For example, attempts might be made to understand the alcohol and drug problems of clients coming to the agency. The evaluator can also search for latent goals of the program as well as potential unintended adverse effects. For example, in an observational study of welfare intake units, the researcher identified several unintended effects of the program on the applicants: embarrassment, misunderstanding, worry, suspicion, and distress.[5]

Collecting information about a program's activities and effects need not be expensive and time consuming. It is not the equivalent of formal research; the data collection procedures are not expected to measure up to scientific standards. The aim is to better inform the evaluator (and hence the program manager) about the program — not to draw conclusions about the nature and amount of its effects. This can be accomplished in various ways: reading actual client files, observing services in the course of their delivery, and interviewing field staff and clients.

PREPARE A PROGRAM MODEL

With the Documents Model, the Manager's Model, and the field work results, the evaluator should now be in a position to identify which program components and which objectives and effects can be seriously considered for inclusion in an evaluation study. The criteria can be summed up as follows:

(a) Program components are well defined and can be implemented in a prescribed manner.

(b) Objectives and effects are clearly specified.

(c) Causal linkages between the program activities and its stated objectives are plausible.

These are preconditions for useful evaluations of program effectiveness. The Program Model reflects them and sets the

stage for a *feasibility* analysis of the proposed evaluation. At
this stage, the evaluation is at least pointed in the right direction. The Program Model thus determines the *possibility* of
certain kinds of evaluation. In other words, an evaluation along
these lines would be appropriate if suitable methodology could
be found and applied at reasonable cost. (Feasibility, as discussed below, addresses this issue of cost in relation to expected benefits from the evaluation.)

Besides providing direction for doing evaluations, evaluability assessment in many cases brings secondary benefits. It
can lead to the program manager giving attention to
shortcomings in program design and delivery, to the restate-
ment of objectives in a clearer fashion, and to more realistic
objectives (fewer unreal ones and possibly fewer unintended
negative effects).

DECIDE KEY QUESTIONS AND THE INFORMATION
NEEDED TO ANSWER THEM

The results of the evaluability assessment enable the manager to decide that key questions should be answered in the
forthcoming evaluation — or in a process of continuing evaluation to be launched. These questions come out of the clarification of the purpose for doing the evaluation — i.e., the types of
decisions that the evaluation is expected to inform. The managerial perspective on evaluation should elicit questions and
information requirements that imply subsequent possible decisions on ways to improve the delivery of program services:
"What will happen if we get the answers?"

The manager and other principal program people should be
able to nominate corresponding key indicators for program
processes as well as outcomes and effects. They can also
suggest appropriate forms of measurement — not in detail, but
in ways that will enable research methods and measurement
tools to be designed and tested. Some indicators may be simple
and quantitative, such as the number of clients seen or counseling sessions conducted. Others may be more complicated, such
as how to measure the redirection of clients' anxiety.

DETERMINE THE FEASIBILITY OF
EVALUATION PROCEDURES

Feasibility of evaluation procedures means considering what we might do and the cost of doing it. The program manager's starting point for assessing the feasibility of implementing an evaluation study is the weighing of its expected benefits, the impact of its probable results.

The manager's perception of future decisions and external interests in the evaluation is based, in general, on the value of the information to be produced. This in turn poses a budgetary question: How much should the manager be willing to pay for getting it?

The evaluability assessment step in the evaluation process sets the stage for decisions about measurement and research design. These obviously have an impact on the final view of the feasibility of any given plan for an evaluation. Is the required information accessible or available? Can the specified data collection procedures be implemented? Would the source of data and the means of collection produce reliable and valid information? Is there a need for sampling participants in the program on some aspect of its implementation? How could this be done? Is there a need for a control or comparison group? How could this be established? Randomly? At what time periods would measurements be taken — before clients' involvement in the program, during it, at its end, somewhat later in time after it was over? What type of data analysis is needed to deal adequately with the manager's information needs? We deal with these issues in the following chapters. Here we simply make the point that the technical requirements should be identified and assessed before they are defined as being feasible in practical terms — that is, during the evaluability assessment.

Finally, the feasibility of an evaluation is affected, as in any other program action, by various constraints that the manager has to keep in mind: for example, shortages of funds, political restrictions, legal limitations on asking certain questions or looking for privileged data, ethical considerations such as might be involved in withholding certain services for the sake of research, and administrative disruptions from an evaluation that might be intolerable. The important thing is not that these contraints appear, but that the manager should try to do something about them.

In some cases, the manager may be able to persuade the legal custodians of information to release it. Or there may be ways of reconciling clients to the withholding of certain services during the evaluation period. Perhaps extra funds can be found to finance the evaluation outside the usual program budget. Political problems may be overcome with suitable persuasion. Program staff may be open to conviction that the benefits of the evaluation will outweigh inconveniences and extra work it will entail for practitioners. On successful application of such remedies, the manager may be able to pursue the evaluation in the optimum way. But, on the other hand, certain constraints may be intractable. To this extent, the evaluation will have to be modified; its environmental constraints are then reflected in research constraints that may limit the usefulness of its ultimate results. With suitable confrontations, the manager may be able to save the proposed evaluation and ensure that it maximizes the scope for practical decisions emanating from it.

CONCLUSIONS

We know from experience that evaluability assessments can increase the probability of achieving useful and credible evaluations. The manager becomes informed, through this preevaluation step, about the extent to which the initial purposes of an evaluation can be achieved. The evaluability assessment improves the terms of reference for the evaluation. It can also lead to many incidental benefits to the manager, facilitating desirable changes in program delivery prior to formal evaluation.

In the next two chapters we move on the important technical questions about doing the evaluation. First, we deal with the information requirements of the exercise — how to get the information that is needed and ensure that it is valid and reliable. Thereafter, we review questions that program managers should deal with on the matter of research design for their evaluations. We assume that the manager will be dealing with technical experts on evaluation — who will have methods to espouse and who will expect decisions on them. An understanding of technical issues of evaluation research and design should put the manager in a better position to make these decisions. Most important, such an understanding enables the manager to ask the right questions and insist on adequate answers. This is good insurance for the quality of the evaluation's ultimate results.

NOTES

1. Carol H. Weiss, "Between the Cup and the Lip," *Evaluation* 1, 2 (1973): 54.
2. R. Bruce Sloane et al., *Psychotherapy vs. Behavioral Therapy* (Cambridge, MA: Harvard University Press, 1975), pp. 145-172.
3. Walter Williams and Richard F. Elmore (eds.) *Social Program Implementation* (New York: Academic Press, 1976).
4. For more detailed instructions on how to carry out evaluability assessments, with examples of problems and solutions, see Leonard Rutman, *Planning Useful Evaluations: Evaluability Assessment* (Beverly Hills, CA: Sage Publications, 1980).
5. Tana Pesso, "Local Welfare Office: Managing the Intake Process," *Public Policy* 26, 2 (1978): 305-330.

Chapter 5

DOING PROGRAM EVALUATION
Measurement

The identification of information requirements and the development of measurement procedures is a central task in program evaluation. The manager plays a key role in identifying the type and volume of information required. He or she should also be involved in selecting or developing the specific measurement procedures. This helps ensure that the evaluators have properly interpreted the information requirements and that the measurement procedures are the most appropriate and reasonable approaches.

AMOUNT AND TYPE OF INFORMATION

Program managers must be involved in establishing the amount and type of information that should be collected. The amount of information should be related to the purpose of the study, the expected use of the findings, and the budget for the evaluation. The temptation, however, is often to collect more information than is really needed. Too much information presents problems. It wastes money. Quality may suffer if rigor and control are compromised because researchers pile up

mountains of unnecessary data. Going after too much information can place (nonproductive) burdens on persons who have
program responsibility delivery if they are expected to implement the measurement procedures. As a consequence, they are
likely to protest against collecting data, do it sloppily, or fail to
meet deadlines.

In regard to the type of information required, we have
organized the discussion around four categories: (1) program,
(2) objectives and effects, (3) antecedent conditions, and (4)
intervening variables.

PROGRAM

Program managers may be interested in using the evaluation
to answer one or more of the following questions: How was the
program implemented? Was it implemented in the prescribed
manner? How does the manner in which the program was
implemented affect the results? What is the most cost-effective
way of operating the program?

In many situations the manager has little idea about what
activities or services are undertaken. For example, a social
welfare department may be providing preventive services to
families through the various district offices. What constitutes
preventive services may vary greatly from district to district.
An evaluation may simply attempt to discover the type of
services offered and the way in which they are provided.

There are different approaches to implementing some programs, and these variations can be identified in advance of an
evaluation. For example, consider the options that exist in
mediation programs designed to settle disputes out of court.

The third party can be a single individual, on occasion someone who is known to the disputants, or the third party can be a
small group of individuals, a "community moot." The specific
functions of the mediator or moot can vary but their general
approach to their mediational task is similar. Both complainant and respondent are given a chance to tell their side of
the story, then discussion ensues between the disputants to
resolve differences. A solution to the dispute, if one is

possible, arises from the discussion; ideally, the solution comes from one of the disputants but it can also be suggested by the mediator, moot, or by friends and relatives who may also be in attendance.[1]

Provision could be made to capture program evaluation along specific dimensions. In the mediation program, plans can be made to collect data on the following: Who served as the third party? How was the discussion structured? What issues were discussed? Who suggested the solution? How was the solution presented? What process led to agreement?

Information on the above questions on program process can serve several purposes. It would be possible simply to describe what took place. There would be evidence on the extent to which the program was implemented in the prescribed manner (if managers expected the practitioners to carry out the program in a particular way). Evaluations could be developed to demonstrate how different ways of implementing the program affect the outcomes. It should be clear that focusing on program process provides the manager with information for use in making program changes.

There are varying levels of detail about program process. The manager must determine the amount of detail needed to serve the purposes of the evaluation. For example, information on parole supervision could involve recording the number and type of supervisory contacts that the parole officer has with the parolee. Added detail could be provided by indicating where the contacts occurred (e.g., at the office of the parole supervisor, at the parolee's home, or at his or her place of employment), the focus of the meeting (e.g., finding a job, dealing with family problems, discussing the social relations of the parolee), contacts with other people on behalf of the client (e.g., employer, welfare agencies, family members). Attempts could be made to examine the nature of their relationship (e.g., determining the extent to which parolees consider their parole officer a "friend" or "police"). Further detail could include monitoring the introduction between parole officer and parolee to reflect the extent to which particular forms of "treatment" or "therapy" were followed.

OBJECTIVES AND EFFECTS

In the previous chapter we showed how to identify and clarify the program's documents, interview managers, and find out what's happening in the field. The manager must decide which objectives and effects should be the focus of the evaluation. In addition, he or she should specify indicators for the objectives and effects to provide evaluators some direction for developing the measurement procedures. For example, what are the indicators of improved mental health? Some possible indicators are: less use of medication, holding a job or being enrolled in training, social relations, and participation in community activities.

Some other approaches to program evaluation do not focus on measuring the attainment of program objectives. For example, goal-free evaluation measures identify the effects of a program, and program effectiveness is judged according to whether the effects adequately address measured needs.[2] Yet we emphasize program objectives in the belief that evaluation studies should address what the program is mandated to achieve — program objectives.

ANTECEDENT CONDITIONS

Antecedent conditions refer to the context within which the program operates, characteristics of the clients served, and background of practitioners. The danger lies in providing an almost endless list of antecedent conditions. For the manager to choose a limited number of important ones, the following questions can serve as a guide: What kind of descriptive background is essential about the context, clients, and practitioners? What antecedent conditions could help explain the program's outcomes? For example, children's IQ might account for the achievements of an educational program. To illustrate antecedent conditions, let us take a training program that aims to increase the employability of the trainees.

Context

- unemployment level in the community
- job opportunities (number and type)
- availability of day care
- remoteness from other urban centers
- industrial make-up of the community
- type of training center (for example, size, or funding)

Clients

- age
- sex
- race
- level of education
- work history
- aptitude

Practitioners (i.e., teachers)

- educational background
- professional versus volunteer
- experience (teaching, in industry, work with similar groups)
- race

Data on antecedent conditions can serve several purposes. As already indicated, such data provide information for interpreting the findings. This can be used to determine if the target group of the program was served by it and to provide clues about the transferrability of the program to other situations. Data on antecedent conditions also make possible analysis to establish what clients benefit most, what types of practitioners produce the best results, and what type of context is most conducive to achieving the program's objectives.

INTERVENING CONDITIONS

Intervening conditions are events or circumstances that arise while the program is being delivered. Some cannot be anticipated in advance of the evaluation (e.g., a sudden increase in employment due to the closing of a large company). Such a closure would obviously limit employment opportunities for graduates of a training program. Unanticipated intervening conditions would be identified and documented during the evaluation.

However, other intervening variables may be foreseen and in such cases could be considered for measurement during the evaluation. For example, clients receiving services from one program may at the same time be involved with several other agencies. The activities of the other agencies are obviously intervening in the sense that they may affect the outcomes. The program may be greatly influenced by the social climate of an organization (e.g., organizational culture and patterns of interaction among different professions and with patients). R. Moos has shown how the nature of the ward environment in a hospital can affect the attainment of treatment objectives. For example, involving patients in ward meetings resulted in them forming committees to welcome new patients and to govern their behavior in the program. The general level of anxiety and depression among both patients and staff declined.[3]

Data on intervening variables help illuminate evaluation findings by identifying the linking or bridging factors between the program and its outcomes. Measuring intervening conditions can provide direction for improving program effectiveness. For instance, certain types of social climate facilitate the accomplishment of program objectives. The program may not require change, but facilitative environments may need to be developed to support the program in achieving its objectives.

HOW TO DEVELOP INDICATORS

In the inventory of information that the manager identified, the meaning of some variables is quite clear and the measures are self-evident. Others are rather vague — e.g., enhanced self-image, improved family relations, and increased employability. It is particularly important to identify indicators for vague variables so as to have direction for the development of appropriate measures. For example, what are the appropriate indicators for the success of parole supervision: (1) arrest, (2) conviction, (3) commitment of 60 days or more, and/or (4) commitment to prison for a longer term? What time period should be used?

The selection indicators serve an important function beyond facilitating the development of appropriate measures. They provide the criteria used to judge the effectiveness of a program. Returning to our parole example, "success" varies from 29.0 percent if "new arrest" is used as the indicator as opposed to 8.7 percent if commitment to prison is used. Changing the time dimension for the selected indicator can also create considerable difference in apparent effectiveness. For example, using "new arrest" as the indicator, the recidivism rate is 29.0 percent after one year, 43.7 percent after two years, and 70.4 percent after six years. Therefore, the rate of recidivism (and the success of parole) could vary from 8.7 percent (prison commitment after one year) to 60.4 percent (arrest after six years).

DATA COLLECTION PROCEDURES AND SOURCES

What type of measurement procedures should be adopted? The purpose of the evaluation and the information requirements of the manager are the starting points for choosing appropriate measurement procedures. In addition, there are other important considerations — available methodology, cost, confidentiality requirements, access to information, and the technical issues of validity and reliability.

In this section we describe the various types of data collection procedures and sources of data. In the next section we discuss the various factors that would influence the choice of which procedures to use in the evaluation.

QUESTIONNAIRES

Information on the selected indicators may be collected through questionnaires designed specifically for this purpose.

They may be administered through face-to-face interviews with respondents, by telephone, or by mail. The format of the questions can vary considerably depending on the purpose and scope of the questionnaire. At one extreme, the questions might be highly structured, leaving little room for the respondent to express his or her opinions freely. For example, the questionnaire might ask for the number of weeks the respondent was employed full-time during the past year, and to rate the job's satisfactions as good, mediocre, or poor. At the other extreme, open-ended questions can invite the respondent (client) to talk freely about the types of problems that brought him or her to the agency and how they feel about any changes brought about through the program. For example, clients could be asked: What do you find interesting about your job gained through the program? In what ways do you feel better or worse off than before?

Highly structured questionnaires, aiming at a predetermined (and limited) amount of specific information have certain advantages — where they can be devised — over the open-ended type. They are easier to administer, code, and analyze. On the other hand, open-ended questions can provide rich detail and insights based on expressions used by respondents.

The manager should ensure that his or her evaluators have checked thoroughly as to the availability and usability of standard questionnaires; these have been previously tested and have a known degree of validity and reliability.

All questionnaires should, of course, be tested on a pilot basis before being accepted for wider use in measuring specified indicators. By contrast, the development of new instruments, particularly the more general, open-ended type, can be costly, time consuming, and often disappointing unless they are very painstakingly prepared and tested. In all cases, the manager will wish to be sure that the instrument chosen or designed will yield the kind and quality of information he or she seeks. This is an important area for managerial inspection and judgment.

OBSERVATIONS AND RATINGS

Observations and ratings of client and practioner activities can be a useful form of measurement. For example, a study measuring activity of old people in residential care employed practitioners who looked for indicators of such activity: Was a subject interacting with another resident (e.g., talking, playing cards, working on joint tasks, making meals, washing dishes, dancing), using recreational materials connected with daily living, performing personal chores (e.g., combing hair, eating, tidying up room, dressing, cleaning), or using items designed to increase mobility (e.g., canes, wheelchairs, walkers). Such observations did not create disruptions for the program and yet permitted measurement in the natural setting where the program operates.

Evaluation studies also sometimes use ratings by professionals or from clients to measure progress in a program. These ratings can be based on interviews with clients, observations by professionals, or reading program files. For example, in a treatment program for alcoholics, the treatment staff members were expected to make a professional judgment about whether the treatment was "successful" or "unsuccessful" — based on whether or not the client achieved "stable abstinence." The judgment about "stable abstinence" depended in part on the length of abstention and in part of the client's attitude ("comfort") with respect to the decision to stop drinking.[6]

In their evaluation of the mediation program referred to earlier, Conner and Surette relied on independent ratings of the out-of-court settlement by the complainant, respondent, and hearing officer. Each rated his or her level of satisfaction with the settlement, on a 7-point scale with the most positive rating equal to 1 ("very satisfied") and the most negative rating equal to 7 ("very unsatisfied").[7]

ORGANIZATIONAL RECORDS AND FILES

Program evaluations can often benefit from data contained in the organization's documents and administrative files. The information was probably not collected originally to serve an evaluation, but it still may be useful for this purpose. For example, a study of interagency coordination in a vandalism prevention project made extensive use of program documents. The types of records examined included letters by program staff to agencies, minutes of meetings, internal memos by program staff to each other on the content of meetings, and letters from agencies to the program.[8]

We believe that recording practices in many programs can be modified to serve evaluation requirements. For example, the intake interview is usually carried out to collect background information on clients and to establish their eligibility for services being offered. This interview, and others like it, can be used to compile much information on antecedent conditions that affect program outcomes. Similarly, along in the process, practitioners can record the services they provide, as an indication of how the program is being implemented. This recording can also capture data on intervening variables and the progress of clients (i.e., the extent to which objectives are being achieved). Interviews at termination of services and follow-up contacts between program staff and clients can often yield valuable information on the outcomes.

Problems of interpretation invariably arise when program documents and files are used for evaluation "inputs" when they have not been designed for this purpose. For example, uniform and systematic recording is needed for the best results in evaluation, but it may not have been insisted on by the manager, in the past. Reports may be late, or parts of them may be missing. And important evaluation information — easily collectible at the time — may not have been collected since there were no provisions for its inclusion in the record.

The foregoing situations reflect a hidden opportunity for improved program management: The manager should consider "building in" the future evaluation data requirement in the program's basic documentation system. Not only can this make future evaluation studies easier to carry out and more conclusive, but it may also be a start on "continuous evaluation" practices by management — with perhaps fewer intermittent special evaluation studies and more frequent opportunities to improve program implementation.[9]

AVAILABLE GOVERNMENT STATISTICS

Available government statistics may, on occasion, also contribute to the fund of evaluation knowledge on a program. Aside from "global statistics" touching on the universe in which the program operates — such as population data, income distribution figures, crime rates, morbidity and death statistics, marriage and divorce rates, child abuse information — data collected by other agencies may be useful in evaluating a given program. For example, a diversion program may be trying to reduce the number of people sentenced to prisons. Data on sentencing practices by judges could be used for analysis of the effectiveness of the diversion program. However, when such data, collected by others, are used in an evaluation, the manager and evaluator have to pay attention to just how the facts were collected and to what meaning can be attached to such measures. This is ensure that program being evaluated avoids the trap of depending on invalid or unreliable data.

SUMMARY

We have reviewed briefly four principal sources of evaluation data — questionnaires, observations and ratings, organizational records and files, and available government statistics. More than one approach can often be used. For example, to evaluate its "hot meals" program for the aged in Charlotte, N.C., management used: (1) agency records to obtain counts of the number of persons served each day, (2) interviews with client-recipients at the meal sites about the quality of the meals they received, and (3) ratings of evaluation office staff and others who acted as trained observers, eating with the recipients and rating both the quality of the meals and the social atmosphere.[10] The use of different approaches permits the comparison of findings according to the data collection procedure used. This helps provide reassurance about the credibility of the findings.

DECISION ISSUES FOR THE MANAGER

Several issues affect the decisions managers (and their evaluators) have to make about data collection procedures and sources: (1) cost, (2) confidentiality of the information desired, (3) reactions of staff, clients or others to the use of questionnaires, (4) validity, and (5) reliability.

COST

Cost is certainly an important consideration in choice of procedures and data sources. Certain kinds of data collection are obviously much more expensive than others. For example, face-to-face interviews are more costly than telephone calls or self-administered questionnaires. A mix of these techniques may be indicated, with key sample data from interviews and confirmation surveys by phone or mail. Studies involving observation are likely to be more costly, for the same reason that face-to-face interviews are — a trained observer has to be engaged to be present to obtain the data. On the other hand, program documents, files, and government statistics can typically be accessed at modest cost.

CONFIDENTIALITY

Confidentiality of the desired data is another important consideration since this may affect access. For example, hospital, medical, or criminal records may be protected from the evaluator's inquiry. Other data may be "commercial-confidential" and be locked away in company files, available only with the permission of the holder. Some programs, such as rape crisis centers, ensure confidentiality to clients; providing information would break this trust. Means can often be found to use data without breaking confidentiality (e.g., presenting aggregate analysis or blanking out names). Nevertheless, confidentiality is a delicate issue deserving careful assessment by the program manager in selecting data collection procedures and sources.

REACTIVITY

Some data collection procedures are more "reactive" than others. For example, administering questionnaires to staff or clients may pose a threat or evoke responses that the respondent thinks the evaluator wishes to hear. In such situations, the very act of carrying out the data collection may affect the behavior the manager is trying to measure. Just asking questions may change attitudes by raising issues in the respondents' minds that they had not been conscious of before. This is a well-known phenomenon in political polls, but it has wider relevance for all kinds of survey research.

On the other hand, program documents, administrative files and government statistics are "nonreactive" sources of evaluation data. The reactivity issue may pose significant constraints on the scope and quality of evaluation data that can be collected. This is a very practical matter, especially when one is considering costly interview programs or other kinds of client surveys.

VALIDITY

Validity is the degree to which a procedure succeeds in measuring what it purports to measure. It is the most important attribute of any data collection procedure. The validity issue appears in several forms.

- *Face validity.* It is obvious, on the face of it, that a proposed procedure is the best way of measuring the phenomenon of interest.

- *Consensus validity.* Several experts agree that this is the way to do it.

- *Content validity.* A test of the data collection instrument indicates that it will produce a reasonable sample of all possible responses, attitudes, behaviors, and so on in what is to be measured.

- *Construct validity.* The degree to which scores on a proposed measure permit inferences about underlying traits, attitudes, behavior probabilities, and the like.

- *Concurrent validity.* Do the scores or responses from the data collection instrument correlate with generally accepted and accurate standards?

- *Predictive validity.* The measure, if applied, can accurately predict something that will take place in the future.[11]

The validity issue arises in many forms and with varying significance. For example, relatively valid measures are available for measuring people's employability. But they are much harder to devise for programs aimed at influencing clients' personalities or future behavior, such as alcoholism, return to crime, tendency to child abuse, or future progress at school of disadvantaged young students. As we have said elsewhere:

> Decisions about whether a study should be conducted, and on what scale, can then be conditioned by the expected degree of validity that could ultimately be attached to the results.[12]

RELIABILITY

Most validity concerns ask the program manager: Are you going to measure the right things? Reliability, on the other hand, poses the complementary question: Are you going to measure them right? The concern of reliability is the suitability of the measurement procedure, the consistency and stability of the measurement(s). Inconsistent and unstable results can all too easily come from a number of different causes: poorly worded questionnaires, variations in the way they are administered, or missing pieces of information. Such imperfections in measurement can lead to biased conclusions about program results. For example, estimated program effects that appear to be small turn out to be large when the analysis is adjusted for measurement error.[13]

The time to consider "reliability" is when evaluations are being planned, not during or after they have been completed and the results have to be reinterpreted so as to fall within the limits of credibility. The manager can do much to ensure reliability in the ensuing evaluation research. This could normally entail some pretest of measurement instruments or precautions (e.g., using several raters to help ensure consistency).

The work of The Urban Institute in developing measures in the field of corrections is quite useful for showing how measures can be identified for objectives, and how the principal data breakouts can be specified along with the means of data collection and source.[14] See Exhibit 5.1 from their report as cited here.

CONCLUSIONS

We reiterate a point emphasized earlier: The purpose of the evaluation and the types of decisions it is expected to support form the starting point for the addressing of measurement issues. The manager should not assume that measurement is too technical a matter to understand. We pointed out that many of the books on developing measurement procedures call for thoughtful consideration of information requirements, the sorting out of the meaning of items of measurement, and the deciding of appropriate and reasonable approaches for data collection. The manager can rely on the expertise of trained researchers to deal with technical matters of validity and reliability, and to prepare the actual data collection procedures. But the manager's role is vital: It invites him or her to raise the right questions and to understand the rationale for procedures proposed by evaluators.

Exhibit 5.1

SUGGESTED OBJECTIVES AND MEASURES FOR MONITORING PRISON
AND PAROLE SERVICES

OBJECTIVES: Incarcerate offenders securely so that they cannot inflict harm on the public, while also providing for the safety, humane treatment, and health of inmates.
Rehabilitate offenders so that they do not commit criminal offenses when released to the community and assist them in becoming socially productive and integrated into the community.

Objective Characteristic	Measures	Principal Data Breakouts	Data Collection Means/Source
To hold securely	1. Annual number of *escapes* divided by annual Average Daily Population (ADP)	Level of security, facility	Analysis of existing escape and prison population records
	2. Number of *crimes committed against the public* ascribed to escapees and to inmates on authorized absence (e.g., work release)	Type of offense, security level	Escape and recapture records and inmate files
	3. Number of incidents of *failure of internal* security, by type of incident, total divided by ADP	Level of security, facility	Special report
	a. Incidents involving *contraband*	Type of contraband	
	b. Incidents of *unrest* by groups of inmates	Type of unrest	
	c. Physical *assaults on prison officials*		

Objective	Measure		Data collection method
To hold humanely	d. Physical assaults on inmates requiring medical treatment		Analysis of existing record
	4. Number of inmate-days of overcrowding	Facility	Trained observer inspections
	5. Rating of sanitation conditions in facilities	Facility	Physical examination of a sample of inmates
	6. Percentage of inmates with unmet health needs	Major facility	
To rehabilitate (changes in attitude)	7. Percentages of inmates with substantial improvement-degradation in attitude associated with criminal or social behavior based on psychological test scales administered at intake and at release; numbers of scales showing significant improvement-degradation	Client-difficulty level	MMPI tests or other psychological exams of random sample of inmates at intake and at discharge
To rehabilitate (reduction in criminal activity)	8. Criminal involvement while under parole	Percentage of all offenders	State criminal justice information network, corrections intake records, FBI RAP sheet follow-up on random sample of parolees
	a. Percentage of all offenaers on parole in the past 12 months who are arrested (or whose arrest passes a preliminary hearing) for a criminal offense allegedly committed prior to completion of parole, or		

(continued)

Exhibit 5.1 Continued

b. Percentage of all offenders on parole in the past 12 months who are *convicted* of a criminal offense that was committed while on parole; or

c. Percentage of all offenders who successfully complete parole *without revocation* for a criminal offense

9. *Criminal involvement when no longer under supervision*

a. Percentage of offenders *arrested* (or whose arrest passes a preliminary hearing) for a criminal offense within 12 months of completion of parole or unconditional discharge; or

b. Percentage of offenders *convicted* for a criminal offense committed within 12 months of completion of parole or unconditional discharge; or

Client-difficulty level

State criminal justice information network, corrections intake records, FBI RAP sheet follow-up on random sample of former inmates

Exhibit 5.1 Continued

Objective	Measure	Data Source
	c. Percentage of offenders *reincarcerated* for a criminal offense within 12 months of completion of parole or unconditional discharge	Corrections agency records, FBI RAP sheets, court records
	10. *Reincarceration:* Number and percentage of offenders entering prison who have previously been incarcerated in the state prison system	
To rehabilitate (increase in social productivity)	11. Percentage of exoffenders *employed* or otherwise socially productive full time when released from parole	Parole agent reports, or special tracking of sample about to be released
	Client employment-difficulty level	

SOURCE: Louis H. Blair et al., *Monitoring the Impact of Prison and Parole Services: An Initial Examination* (Washington, DC: The Urban Institute, 1977). ©1977 by The Urban Institute. Reprinted by permission.

NOTES

1. Ross F. Conner and Ray Surette, "Processing Citizens' Disputes Outside the Courts," *Evaluation Review* 4, 6 (December 1980): 741.

2. M. Scriven, "Evaluation Bias and its Control," in G. V Glass (ed.) *Evaluation Studies Review Annual,* Vol. 1 (Beverly Hills, CA: Sage Publications, 1976), pp. 119-139.

3. Rudolph H. Moos, *Evaluating Treatment Environments* (New York: John Wiley, 1974), p. 117.

4. P. Hoffman and Barbara Stone-Meierhoefer, *Reporting Recidivism Rates: The Criterion/Followup Issue,* Report 19 (Washington, DC: United States Parole Commission, March 1978), p. 7.

5. David Felce et al., "Measuring Activity of Old People in Residential Care: Testing a Handbook for Observers," *Evaluation Review* 4, 3 (June 1980): pp. 371-387.

6. Roger G. Dunham and Armand L. Nauss, "Evaluation of Treatment Programs, *Evaluation Quarterly* 3, 3 (August 1979): 415.

7. Ross F. Conner and Ray Surette, "Processing Citizens' Disputes Outside the Court," p. 754.

8. Eugene Walsh Flaherty, Ellen Barry, and Marshall Swift, "Use of an Unobtrusive Measure for the Evaluation of Inter-Agency Coordination," *Evaluation Quarterly* 2, 2 (May 1978): 261-273.

9. For a more detailed discussion, see The Urban Institute, *Developing Client Monitoring Systems, A Guide for State and Local Social Service Agencies* (Washington, DC: U.S. Department of Health and Human Services, Office of Human Development Services, 1981); and also a companion brochure, *Administrator's Guide to Social Service Client Outcome Monitoring.*

10. Harry P. Hatry, Richard E. Winnie, and Donald M. Fisk, *Practical Program Evaluation for State and Local Governments* (Washington, DC: The Urban Institute, 1981), p. 66.

11. For a detailed discussion of validity, see Jim C. Nunnally and Robert L. Durham, "Validity, Reliability and Special Problems of Measurement in Evaluation Research," in Elmer L. Struening and Marcia Guttentag, *Handbook of Evaluation Research* (Beverly Hills, CA: Sage Publications, 1975), pp. 289-354.

12. Leonard Rutman, *Planning Useful Evaluations: Evaluability Assessment* (Beverly Hills, CA: Sage Publications, 1980), p. 68. For a specific case illustrating some of the complexities of the validity issue, see Sol L. Garfield and Richard M. Prager, "Evaluation of Outcome in Psychotherapy," *Journal of Consulting and Clinical Psychology* 37, 3 (1971): 307-313.

13. See Robert F. Boruch and David Rindskopf, "On Randomized Experiments, Approximations to Experiments, and Data Analysis," in Leonard Rutman (ed.) *Evaluation Research Methods: A Basic Guide* (Beverly Hills, CA: Sage Publications, 1977), p. 165.

14. Louis H. Blair et al., *Monitoring the Impacts of Prison and Parole Services: An Initial Examination* (Washington, DC: The Urban Institute, 1977), pp. 2-3, 12.

Chapter 6

DOING PROGRAM EVALUATION
Research Design

Research design has two central concerns. Did the program produce the measured results *(attribution)?* To what extent are the results of the evaluation relevant for situations (i.e., places, clients, and circumstances) other than those studied in the research *(generalizability)?* In this chapter we elaborate on the meaning and importance of attribution and generalizability. We then present various research designs for doing program evaluation. This discussion should facilitate the choice in research designs suited to the purpose of the evaluation (which includes considerations of attribution and generalizability), tempered by available funds and constraints.

ATTRIBUTION — A MATTER OF CONFIDENCE

Research designs must be examined in relation to how much confidence they provide that the measured accomplishments of the program were in fact produced by the program. Or were they affected by extraneous events? In the terminology of program evaluators, are there threats to internal validity that the research design can rule out? For example, the (measured)

increases in the earnings of the graduates of a manpower training program might be attributable to such nonprogram factors
as negotiated settlements for higher wages, an atypically good
group of enrollees who would have done well even without the
training, or the fact that those experiencing difficulties dropped
out before the program was completed (and were not followed
up in the evaluation). In such evaluations — where attribution
is a major concern — properly designed studies can help rule
out extraneous factors. They aim to leave the program as the
only plausible explanation for whatever measured results are
analyzed and reported.

The importance of the attribution issue can vary from one
evaluation to another. Attribution is not a major issue in studies
that aim to determine whom the program reached and to document how the program was implemented. The aim may also be
to identify outcomes and not primarily to establish the program's contribution to their achievement. The main purpose of
the evaluation may be simply to document changes over time.

GENERALIZABILITY — A MATTER OF REPRESENTATIVENESS

On generalizability, the question is whether or not the nature and scope of the research allows its results to be related to
situations not covered by that research. This might be, for
example, its relevance to other populations, organizational settings, community contexts and geographical locations.

The issue of generalizability varies in importance with the
purpose for doing an evaluation. For example, generalizability
is not of major concern where the evaluation is only expected to
serve the manager in making program changes, particularly of
relatively small programs serving the entire eligible population
of a restricted area. In such a situation, the specific study may
not be expected to contribute to knowledge to the field as a
whole or possible program changes elsewhere.

Demonstration projects. Generalizability is the whole point
of demonstration projects that implement a proposed new program in one or a few locations, or on a small scale, to test its

effectiveness. Guaranteed annual income experiments are a case in point. Generalizability was a major concern as the key evaluation questions were those pertaining to its implementation as a permanent national program.

Very large programs. When the evaluation can cover only a small portion of the sites where the program is delivered or of the clients covered by a very large program, generalizability becomes a central issue in research design. Evaluation of unemployment insurance programs is an example. Evaluations of interventions introduced to the program (such as different eligibility criteria) need to include a representative group of clients, regions and district offices if program-wide generalizations are expected.

Knowledge-building studies. Evaluations are often undertaken to contribute toward the knowledge base in particular fields. For example, there are numerous evaluations of treatment programs for the mentally ill. The generalizability concerns have to do with: how the treatment was delivered, what type(s) of mental problem was treated, characteristics of the patients, nature of the treatment setting, who provided the service, and so on. Generalizability requirements can then be met by structuring program delivery. For example, there may be insufficient data on a program's effectiveness with clients from a particular social class and/or experiencing particular problems. An evaluation could be designed to involve such clients in the program so that findings can be generalized to them, adding to the body of knowledge about the intervention.

The selection of a particular design is based on the purpose of the evaluation, program circumstance, cost, and other constraints (political, legal, ethical, and administrative). The research design issues are: the structure and delivery of the program, the number of measurement points used in the evaluation, the creation of comparison and control groups, the need for correct sampling, and the challenge to maintain a normal situation in the program during the evaluation.

These subjects take up the rest of this chapter. Some of the material may seem complicated. The program manager should be able to depend on professional evaluators to steer a proper course. Our purpose is to alert the manager to the nature and significance of the research design matters discussed. He or she will at least be able to ask the right questions. Successful research design depends a lot on common sense in handling technical matters for the pursuit of a declared evaluation purpose. We are confident that most program managers can exercise judgment without undue difficulty, even in the abstruse labyrinths of state-of-the-art methodology.

SORTING OUT THE IMPACT OF
PROGRAM COMPONENTS

The program manager may wish to focus his or her attention on the impact of one or more specified components of the program. This poses problems of research design where the program is made up of several components (as we described this situation in Chapter 1). They are all expected to contribute to the same designated objective(s) of the program. For example, restitution programs to discourage criminals from committing future offenses involve making them pay for their crimes. In addition to the component of paying restitution (in money or community services), the program may include other components such as counseling for family problems, treatment for alcoholism or drug addiction, help in finding a job, or assistance with housing problems — all aiming to reduce recidivism. Questions that should be asked include: How much does each component contribute to the overall objective? Could some be eliminated without materially affecting the outcome? Which might be stepped up? What combination of potential services produces the best results in heading off future trouble with the law?

A multifaceted program poses questions of research design in evaluation. Two areas are factorial design and the use of statistical controls.

FACTORIAL DESIGN

One research design involves setting up the evaluation by restructuring the delivery of the program. In this scenario, clients receive differing combinations of the treatment. For example, all clients would be involved in some type of restitution. Under a selected random assignment procedure, some clients would also use one or more of the other services — i.e., family counseling, treatment for alcoholism or drug addiction, assistance in finding a job or housing. This could be done according to the site of the services. Or, in any one place, recipients could be screened to receive one of a number of combinations of the services. In this design, the factors affecting program outcomes are differentiated, component by component. Result: information on what works and what does not.

STATISTICAL CONTROLS

An alternative to factorial design is to allow recipients of the services to select their own mix of program offerings — perhaps guided by program professionals on a case-by-case basis. Statistical analysis might then be able to determine the connection between involvement in a particular service(s) and the results from this self-selection option. The attractiveness of such an approach is that the program is not altered for the sake of the evaluation. However, the reasons for being involved in some components and not in others are related to differences between clients. Therefore, the success or failure of a component may be primarily related to the characteristics of the clients who chose (or were referred to) particular services.

TESTING ALTERNATIVE IMPLEMENTATION APPROACHES

Earlier we emphasized the point that programs can often be implemented in many ways. The program manager can use an evaluation to test different ways of delivering the program's services. The results will likely differ. Or the manager may be interested in the outcomes of the program being implemented in a certain manner. In either case, where the concern is with testing a particular approach to program implementation, the research design requires the program manager to stabilize the delivery mechanism during the time period being evaluated —

so that impacts can be related to an implementation process that is known and representative of the prescribed approach.

The use of factorial designs as described above and the stabilizing of program delivery help ensure attribution of the measured outcomes to a particular program component(s) implemented in a prescribed manner. Yet such controls over the design and delivery of the program may result in such a contrived situation that the findings have little relevance for the "real" world. In other words, a research design that is considered strong in relation to the attribution issue may be weak for purposes of generalizability. These are the tradeoffs that the manager must consider in determining the research design best suited to the purpose of the evaluation.

USING GROUP VERSUS SINGLE-SUBJECT DESIGNS

Program evaluations normally study the impact of the program on a group of many people. Findings indicate how well the clients fared on common outcome measures. An alternative approach is to focus the measuring and analysis of change on individuals. Measures of outcome are designed for each client and progress is individually monitored.

GROUP DESIGNS

Evaluations that use group designs assume common problems and expected changes for clients; impacts are similarly amenable to aggregate analysis. Such programs may have standardized methods of impact measurement, for example: grades achieved, type of job obtained, amount of income earned, number of rehabilitated alcoholics, and so on. Evaluation data in such programs can be grouped and averaged to find central tendencies and variations. The data reveal "movement" that occurs when the program's interventions are directed to clients with specified needs or problems. This is the usual situation, and this chapter essentially deals with group designs. However, the single-subject designs may be considered to be the desired approach by the program manager. We therefore provide a brief discussion of such designs.

SINGLE-SUBJECT DESIGNS

Some programs operate on a special assumption — that each individual they are serving has unique problems and requires an individualized intervention. This means that outcomes will vary, client by client. It does not make sense to group all these people and apply statistical analysis to them as a group of clients.

Michael Patton has commented on the usefulness of using individual outcomes for community mental health centers that aim to increase clients' "independence":

It is possible to construct a test which can be administered to a large group of people measuring their relative degrees of independence. Indeed, such tests exist; these typically ask what kind of activities a person engages in and takes responsibility for, such as personal hygiene, transportation, initiatives in social interaction, food preparation, and so on. In many programs measuring such criteria in a standardized fashion provides the information that program staff would like to have. However, in programs that emphasize individualization of treatment and outcomes, program staff may argue, quite justifiably, that independence has a different meaning for different people under different life conditions. Thus, for example, for one person independence may have to do with a changing family dynamic and changed relationships with parents. For another person, independence may have to do with nonfamilial relationships — that is, interactions with persons of the opposite sex, social activities, and friendships. For still other clients the dominant motif in independence may have to do with the employment and economic factors. For still others it has to do with learning to live alone. While clients in each case may experience a similar psychotherapeutic process, the meaning of the outcomes for their personal lives will be quite different. What program staff want to document under such conditions is the unique meaning of the outcomes for each client. [1]

There are different approaches to the use of single-subject designs. Some are very much related to a particular form of treatment such as behavior modification and monitor changes in client behavior when a treatment is introduced, reduced, or magnified.[2]

One widely adopted approach is Goal Achievement Scaling. It calls for identification of a unique set of goals for each client — as opposed to the definition of general program goals for the clients as a whole. Here is an example of a goal-attainment scale constructed for an unemployed person.

Column 1	Column 2	Column 3
Worst outcome expected	Unemployed and not in job training	−2
Less than expected outcome	Unemployed but in job training	−1
Expected outcome	Part-time employment and in job training	0
More than expected outcome	Full-time employment and earning less than $125/wk	1
Best outcome expected	Full-time employment and earning more than $125/wk	2

The goal-attainment scale is constructed as follows:

After a particular goal is decided upon, a scale is formed which details the relative positive and negative outcomes which could reasonably be expected of this client. For example, if enhancing job performance were the goal, the scale might resemble . . . column 2. In order to make the individualized scales as comparable as possible across clients or programs, anchor points from worst anticipated outcome to most positive outcome are used as a template in specifying individualized GAS scale points (see column 1). . . . As indicated in column 2, . . . the goal setter writes down specific values (usually behavioral) which would be considered measures of the various levels of outcome for a particular client on a particular goal. Although five scale points are usually recommended, only two points are absolutely necessary for construction of a GAS scale. Finally to do statistical analyses some numerical value must be assigned to each of the scale points. Column 3 depicts five values which are often used. It is also possible to give more importance to certain scales by multiplying the scales by different weights.[3]

Goal-attainment scaling appears attractive as both a clinical and evaluative tool. Yet as Calsyn and Davidson point out, goal-attainment scaling has problems: on "reliability" (low levels of agreement between different raters on the meaning of the client's stated goals) and on "validity" (a lack of correspondence between the results of measuring instruments that purport to measure the same thing, i.e., a change in client situation). Moreover, goals set by clients, or with the help of therapists, may not always be consistent with the goals envisaged by the legislators who approved the funding of the program.[4]

Goal-attainment scaling, like other approaches, may be flawed. Too often managers adopt an approach to evaluating programs without a sufficient understanding of the strengths and weaknesses. No approach is likely to be perfect in meeting the manager's needs. However, the manager can be helped to make an informed choice by receiving an analysis of the various approaches so that he or she can choose the one best suited to the purpose of the evaluation.

The program manager has to decide on the balance between "group" and "individual" measures of program achievement. Compromises may be feasible, such as aggregated analyses of group effects with a suitable number of individual-based evaluations to qualify the more broadly based research. In other words, it may not be a black-and-white decision. Research design presents an opportunity for the program manager to exercise initiative based on an intimate comprehension of the entire program and on the expected use of the information.

SELECTING THE NUMBER OF MEASUREMENT POINTS

One of the most common research designs is one in which measurement of change takes place after clients have finished the program. These evaluations typically measure "client satisfaction" with services or "perceived benefits" from the program. Without a baseline measure of the clients' situation before involvement with the program, it is difficult to establish objectively whether change occurred. In some instances, the evaluator may be able to develop "pseudo before-measures" by asking clients about their situation prior to involvement wtih the program. However, the validity and reliability of this is usually problematic in relation to attitudinal and behavioral measures.

Evaluations that aim to document change should have before-and-after measures of any changes that the program attempts brought to produce. Symbolically:

$$O_1 \; X \; O_2$$

where O_1 is the situation *before* the program's intervention(s), X represents the program's activities, and O_2 is an observation on the situation some time *after* the occurrence of the intervention. This is a very simple representation of measurement point selection. If it were used in an evaluation, it might not be adequate. For example, a family service bureau providing counseling services may pursue the objective of improving family functioning. The therapists could document the before situation by having family members rate themselves on a seven-point scale for such factors as fights, activities undertaken together, feelings of closeness, and so on. Assuming improvement occurred between the before and after measures, the manager faces questions of attribution. Was the effect produced by the program, or was it mainly brought about by influences not connected with the program? Some possibilities:

- *Selection.* The program happened to attract highly motivated people who struggled with and solved their family problems, and would have done so without the help of the program.

- *Maturation.* People over time developed the capacity to solve their problems, independent of the program designed to help them.

- *Regression*. The improvement observed is the continuation of a trend that existed for months prior to the clients' involvement in the program.

- *Historical factors*. The introduction of new services such as day care, not part of the program, accounted for the improvement observed.

- *Mortality*. People not being helped by the program dropped out of it and were not included in the follow-up observations and evaluation analysis.[5]

The above simple design, with only two observations points, might be strengthened through the use of multiple before measures:

$$O_1 \quad O_2 \quad O_3 \quad O_4 \quad X \quad O_5$$

Under this design, the manager has a better knowledge of the progress (or lack of it) of the program's clients before they became involved in the program. This, in turn, would make it easier to identify the linkages between program services and the after changes observed in the clients — any break in an observable trend might be legitimately attributable to the intervention of the program.

The graph in Exhibit 6.1 shows a rising trend of commitments to mental hospitals up to 1980, when the community-based mental health program was implemented. After 1980, the trend is reversed — so that in the absence of other causes, the improvement could be attributed to the program. Such a design has obvious advantages over a simple before-and-after measurement. It is possible to establish whether changes are simply the continuation of a trend rather than an improvement. Yet this design does not rule out historical factors that may have intervened to produce the change. Of course, if the evaluation were planned and carried out in 1982, as in the example, one might not be able to find enough historical data to plot as many before observations as might be desired to maximize the attribution quality of the results.

Exhibit 6.1

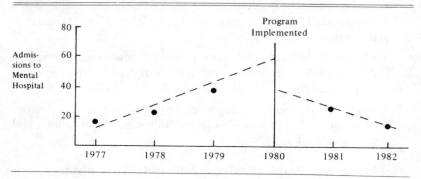

USING COMPARISON AND CONTROL GROUPS
IN EXPERIMENTS

Research designs can usually be strengthened — that is, for making cause-and-effect inferences — by the addition of *comparison* or *control* groups. The evaluation's experimental group consists of those recipients of program services whose situation is being evaluated. The control group either receives no services, or different ones, during the period of the evaluation research.

A commonly used research design is one that makes postprogram comparisons between an experimental group and a nonequivalent comparison group:

$$\frac{X\ O_1}{O_1}$$

For example, achievement tests are administered to children who have completed a Head Start program. For purposes of comparison, the same tests are given to children considered to be similar to those who participated in the program (e.g., socioeconomic status, race, ethnicity, and so on). Differences in achievement are then considered to be due to the impact of the program. However, here we have no baseline to establish the amount and type of improvement that may have occurred through the program. Moreover, we cannot rule out the many threats to internal validity, especially the probable initial differences between the two groups (selection). They are referred to as *nonequivalent groups* because they were not established through random assignment procedures.

Another type of design, referred to as a *quasi-experiment,* would be of the form:

$$\frac{0_1 \; X \; 0_2}{0_1 \; X \; 0_2}$$

Here, we have before and after measures for the experimental group receiving program services (top line) and a nonequivalent group of nonrecipients (bottom line). For example, people who are unemployed may be referred to manpower training through the local employment center. They would constitute the experimental group. A comparison group could be established by locating people on unemployment insurance with characteristics as those who received training; that is, the groups are similar in such respects as age, sex, occupation, past employment record, earnings, and so on. Before and after measures on such factors as employability and earnings would be undertaken for both groups.

The main advantage of this design over the earlier ones is that it can rule out some nonprogram factors that can account for the measured outcomes — e.g., changes in employment opportunities — since both groups could be expected to be equally affected by this situation. The principal drawback could be, however, that the groups are in fact significantly *different.* The differences might be in known factors such as employability and past earnings or in unknown factors such as aptitudes and motivation. The challenge to the evaluator is to minimize this problem through proper research design — since such differences could just as well account for the success of the training.

The *experimental design* is generally considered to be the strongest for making attribution of cause and effect. It takes the following form:

$$\frac{0_1 \; X \; 0_2}{0_1 \quad\; 0_2}$$

The difference between this design and some of the others described above lies in the manner in which the experimental and control groups are established — through randomization procedures. Randomization entails the use of assignment procedures where chance is what determines the composition of experimental and control groups. These groups are therefore assumed to be similar on both known (and measured) variables such as age or past earnings as well as unknown (and unmeasured) variables such as attitudes or skills. Since it is assumed that groups are equivalent, we have ruled out selection problems along with other threats to internal validity.

We have numerous examples of experimental designs used to evaluate social programs.[7] These examples point out the feasibility of using experimental designs. There are many arguments against randomization that point out the difficulties or even the impossibility of employing it. Many of the arguments have to do with public relations — that is, how to explain the use of random assignment to establish eligibility when need or merit should determine who receives the service. Other arguments focus on the ethics of denying some people service. Yet programs often have waiting lists, so that the means of establishing eligibility becomes the issue, not the denial of service per se. Moreover, it is presumed that the service is beneficial and yet this is what the evaluation aims to establish. An experiment need not entail denial of service but may instead be used for comparing alternative programs.

We are not proposing experimental designs as a panacea for all situations. The purpose of the evaluation may not call for unequivocal causal inferences. Findings already established for some programs may be used for comparison. There may be too few clients to have experimental and control groups. The approach may be too expensive. Statutory obligations to provide service to qualifying clients may make experiments impossible. The organization's professionals may be hard to convince. The public relations problems may be too great. And the experimental design that creates "focus inequities" (i.e., some clients participate in the program and others do not) may bring about changes in clients and staff that end up creating new threats to internal validity (such as overcompensation or demoralization).

The challenge is to select a research design that is best suited to the purpose of the evaluation. We have presented options and indicated their strengths and weaknesses. The manager should consider these options in light of such concerns as: (1) the extent to which the information for decision making requires relatively unequivocal findings about cause and effect, (2) the funds available, (3) the time frame for the evaluation, and (4) constraints — political legal, ethical, administrative, and professional.

SAMPLING TO HELP ENSURE REPRESENTATIVENESS

A program may be established for the purpose of having it evaluated, or program modifications may be introduced for testing. In these situations, sampling needs to be considered as a means of involving clients in the experimental group. Determining where to establish the program and who should be involved are major considerations affecting the generalizability of evaluation findings.

For example, a Board of Education may be interested in the effectiveness of computer-assisted instruction. It may be interested in doing evaluations of this before deciding on wholesale introduction. What schools should be involved? Which grades? Which classrooms? What courses? How many children? The intended use of the findings is the basis for answering these questions. The program manager must be clear about the types of decisions that the evaluation is expected to inform to ensure that appropriate sampling procedures are used for deciding where the experimental program should be located and who should be involved.

Once choices have been made about program participation, sampling should be considered in relation to the scope of data collection. Evaluations of programs that serve many areas and numerous clients need not include everyone in the data collection. Sampling procedures can be used to select locations, clients, and time periods (e.g., hours or days during certain designated periods).

Sampling is an important means of reducing costs in program evaluation. It also helps minimize the disruptions in program delivery and lessen the burden placed on practitioners involved in data collection and other aspects of the evaluation effort. The basis for making sampling decisions is the level of generalizability that the evaluation is expected to produce.

MAINTAINING THE NATURAL SITUATION

Maintaining the natural operating situation of the program is an essential ingredient of evaluations where generalizability is a major concern. Program managers must recognize that the implementation of evaluation often creates a highly fabricated, or artificial, situation — which limits the generalizability of findings. Consider the guaranteed annual income experiment. In the initial experiments, the guarantee period was three years. Would people react differently to the three-year program than to one they believed was permanent? The experiment received a lot of media coverage. Did the attention given it influence the behavior of the experimental group? The evaluation entailed close monitoring of the clients' income level and work activities: Did the monitoring itself affect the clients?

Many experimental programs use professionals who are enthusiastic about the intervention being pursued. Does their enthusiasm influence the outcomes? Similarly, programs vary in the extent to which clients choose a service (e.g., employment placement) or are somewhat coerced to participate (e.g., parole). Does the client's interest in the program and basis of participation influence the effectiveness of the program in achieving its objectives?

The expected use of the findings should influence the evaluation design, so that it is as representative as possible of the situation to which the findings will be generalized and used. Otherwise, the risk is that the findings have little validity for the real world in which the program manager will be introducing changes. Findings that are considered quite unequivocal in attributing cause and effect may have little relevance for managerial action if they cannot be generalized for future decision making.

CONCLUSIONS

Many types of research design can be considered, and should be considered, in the planning of an evaluation. We have pointed out that the purpose of the evaluation study is the starting point for selecting its research design. A major consideration is whether or not the evaluation aims for unequivocal conclusions about the program's contribution to the achievement of its stated objectives and effects. Decisions regarding the timing of measurement, use of control or comparison groups, and the means of establishing them take on added importance when the evaluation is to draw causal inferences about program impact. Similarly, the use of sampling procedures and maintaining a natural situation have to be related to the requirements for generalizability and the cost of attaining it.

The art of program evaluation lies in the tailoring of research design to the purposes of the evaluation in a way that is affordable and realistic in terms of real-world constraints. This means the creative use of techniques harmonized with the environment of their application. It is the recipe for evaluations that are credible and relevant to the practical decisions of program management.

NOTES

1. M. Patton, *Qualitative Evaluation Methods* (Beverly Hills, CA: Sage Publications, 1980), p. 63.

2. Michael W. Howe, "Casework Self-Evaluation: A Single-Subject Approach," *Social Service Review*, 48, 1 (March 1974): 1-23.

3. Robert J. Calsyn and William S. Davidson, "Do We Really Want a Program

Evaluation Strategy Based Solely on Individualized Goals? A Critique of Goal Attainment Scaling," *Evaluation Studies Review Annual,* Vol. 3, p. 702.

4. Ibid., p. 711.

5. T. D. Cook and D. T. Campbell, "The Design and Conduct of Quasi-Experiments in Field Settings," in Marvin D. Dunnette (ed.) *Organizational Psychology* (Chicago: Rand McNally, 1965), pp. 223-325.

6. Robert F. Boruch, A. John McSweeney, and E. Jon Soderstrom, "Randomized Field Experiments for Program Planning, Development and Evaluation," *Evaluation Quarterly* 2, 4 (November 1978): 655-695.

7. Robert F. Boruch, A. John McSweeny, and E. Jon Soderstrom, "Randomized Field Experiments for Program Planning, Development, and Evaluation: An Illustrative Bibliography," *Evaluation Quarterly* 2, 4 (November 1978): 655-695.

Chapter 7

USING EVALUATIONS FOR DECISION MAKING

MANAGE THE EVALUATION FOR "ACTIONABLE RESULTS"

If evaluations are to be used for decision making they have to be planned from the beginning with this end in mind. We have already emphasized this point on a number of occasions in this book. Ideally, the evaluation design should provide for constructive — not just negative or laudatory — comments and directions for better means of program delivery. Linking program processes to outcomes serves this purpose. It also makes the manager's implementation tasks much easier. In this chapter, we complete the themes of Chapter 3, with the final step in evaluation, using its results. Even with good preparation, getting value for evaluation dollars is not always easy.

BE AWARE OF THE BARRIERS TO THE PRACTICAL USE OF EVALUATION RESULTS

Program managers should make a realistic assessment of barriers to the use of evaluation results before preparing their implementation plans. Carol Weiss has provided a useful perspective on this problem.[1] She has noted how some evaluators consider themselves academically "above" any involvement in securing improvements in program delivery. Many prefer to "write and run," possibly knowing that they are not equipped to deal with the sometimes vexing problems of implementation. From our standpoint, this means that early managerial control over the evaluation is doubly important. The manager's overriding objective is to see that the evaluation produces directions for change rather than merely arms-length observations about the nature of program successes and failures. Even if the evaluators are unwilling or unable to contribute to implementation of changes, good project management can set the manager up with issues of program redirection within his or her competence and authority.

In Chapter 3, we also recommended a reporting plan and managerial control that would produce illuminating — not obfuscatory — final reports from the evaluators. If the final report on the evaluation is properly planned and directed (not left to the experts), it should contain suitable summary material focused on *what should be done*. Failure to achieve this important report control can present a barrier to implementation to a manager interested in learning about new directions for planning and improvements in certain details of program management.

Organizational factors may pose problems for the implementation of evaluation results. Many organizations are inherently resistant to change; organizational survival is a primary goal.

Program practitioners may be reluctant to change their ways of doing things, as a matter of professional pride. People with long attachments to the program and their work in it may feel they have to "keep the faith" even in the face of countervailing beliefs and empirical evidence. Politically, the organization may be part of a larger policy scenario where political realities fence in the manager's innovative scope and remedial power. We have urged that problems such as these should be faced early in the evaluation-planning process so that they do not spring up unexpectedly at the end and negate much of the value of the evaluation effort.

Aside from the foregoing institutional constraints on results and implementation, the logical implications of the evaluation may pose decisions that the manager cannot tolerate. They may be both too costly and too disruptive in any number of ways. Implementing items on a "wish list" of recommendations may be simply impractical. Our point in all this is that implementation problems of an institutional and practical nature need to be ventilated before decisions are made about how and when evaluation results will be used.

SET PRIORITIES FOR ACTION ON IMPLEMENTATION

The manager uses the completed evaluation as a foundation for *managerial planning,* with priorities for selected actions. Our position is that this is much easier to do when the evaluation has been carried out with the active and sympathetic participation and involvement of key program staff members — each of whom will likely develop interests and commitments to some aspect of the forthcoming results. At the end of the evaluation research, the manager has several options, each with its cadre of supporters and potential implementers.

The next step for the manager is to establish specific timetables, priorities, and resource allocations for implementation (having in mind whatever constraints obtain). This does not mean doing the most important things first. Some simple implementation actions can be scheduled for immediate application. More time and planning may be needed for those of a more intricate nature, perhaps involving a sequence of actions where the chain of implementation logic might be broken by the latest implementation effort. In any event, the first step is to set the priorities for action.

Once the priorities have been set, the manager develops a timetable, a month-by-month schedule of the implementation actions. The timing is critical: If projects are not put firmly on a calendar, slippage in their accomplishment is almost certain to follow.

DEFINE AND IMPLEMENT IMPROVEMENT PROJECTS

Each implementation is a "project," a set of planned actions with a starting and finishing date, a manager to look after them, and a budget of manpower and money.[2] The matter of personal responsibility, authority, and accountability is critical. Assigning them is a must for the program manager; otherwise, nothing may happen because no one can be held accountable for the decided actions.

The manager's next step in implementation is to supply the implementers with the resources needed and to launch them on their work at the appointed starting date.

MONITOR AND CONTROL PROJECT PROGRESS

Project monitoring for successful implementation is a key role for the manager. He or she can make changes, shift timetables and priorities, or approve successful execution of plans. Such control is especially necessary where substantial sums of money and manpower are involved and where the timetable is critical because of its implications for other events in the program.

FEED BACK THE RESULTS OF IMPLEMENTATION

Many of the results of implementation will suggest consideration of further changes in the program's components, procedures and delivery mechanisms. This is natural. It is the continuing influence of evaluation on planning. Indeed, planning and evaluation are opposite sides of the same coin, one looking ahead and the other looking back for guidelines on the future. The close connection, and the universally recognized place of planning in the functions of management, brings us back again to the notion that evaluation should be viewed as an ongoing, continuous process for seeking improvements in program delivery.

NOTES

1. Carol H. Weiss, *Evaluation Research* (Englewood Cliffs, NJ: Prentice-Hall, 1972), pp. 110-128.

2. Various scheduling techniques are available. A set of activities can be charted on the rows of a matrix, with lines indicating the starting and finishing dates of each activity under columns that indicate, say, weeks on the implementation calendar. More sophisticated networking techniques can be useful where project activities are related to one another in complex ways. See, for example, Richard I. Levin and Charles A. Kirkpatrick, *Planning and Control with PERT/CPM* (New York: McGraw-Hill, 1966), a basic text.

APPENDIX

Exercise on Planning Program Evaluations

Here are four program "case summaries" for readers to use in exercises on the planning of program evaluations. References indicate sources for additional information if needed. As a guide, we have included 26 questions on various aspects of evaluation planning. They range from identifying uses and purpose, through measurement and research design, to utilization of the results. Program managers should find these exercises helpful as a warm-up for planning an evaluation of their own program and for reinforcing propositions we have made in this book. Students of program evaluation and their university instructors should also find them helpful as part of a course on program evaluation.

EXERCISE ON PLANNING PROGRAM EVALUATIONS

IDENTIFYING USES AND PURPOSE

(1) Identify the potential users of evaluation findings, indicating how they could use evaluation findings.

(2) What types of decisions could the evaluation contribute toward for the program manager?

(3) What questions would the evaluation have to answer to help the program manager make the identified decisions?

PROGRAM ANALYSIS

(4) List the elements of program structure under the following categories:

Program Components   *Outputs*   *Objectives/Effects*

(5) Develop a documents model of the program.

(6) Role-play an interview with the program manager and pose the questions to assist in development of a program manager's model of the program. (Alternatively, assume that such an interview occurred and respond to the questions normally asked of the manager.)

(7) Develop a program manager's model of the program.

(8) Is there a need to do a field visit to find out what's really happening? If yes, indicate how this visit would be conducted, indicating what you would examine.

(9) Synthesize your understanding of program structure by preparing an evaluable program model.

(10) What is the significance in the changes from one program model to another?

(11) Specify which program components will be addressed in the evaluation study.

PURPOSE

(12) Does the program analysis conducted result in changes to the initial purpose(s)? How?

(13) Are the initial questions still relevant? Should some be deleted? New questions?

MEASUREMENT

(14) List the variables that the evaluation should include under the following categories:

   Antecedent   Program   Intervening   Objectives/Effects

(15) Select some of the variables that you consider major and identify indicators that reflect the meaning of the objective or effect.

(16) What data sources or data-collection procedures would you use for measuring: (a) program process and (b) outcomes?

(17) Assess the cost implications of the data collection procedure(s).

(18) Are there any major constraints affecting data collection?

(19) What are the major validity issues likely to be encountered? How would you minimize these problems of validity?

(20) What are the major reliability issues likely to be encountered? How would you minimize these problems of reliability?

RESEARCH DESIGN

(21) Present the research design that you would use, indicating:
    (a) sampling methods (if relevant);
    (b) whether control or comparison groups will be used;
    (c) how control or comparison groups would be elaborated;
    (d) timing of measurement.

(22) What major constraints will likely affect the implementation of this research design?

(23) Assess the strengths and weakness of the design in relation to:
    (a) internal validity (causal conferences)
    (b) external validity (generalizability)

(24) Develop an Administrative Agreement between the evaluator and manager. In other words, specify obligations of each party.

UTILIZATION

(25) What factors are likely to impede or facilitate the use of findings?

(26) What actions would you take to help ensure that the findings are considered and utilized for decision making?

INDEPENDENCE WORKSHOP[1]

The Independence Workshop is a training facility for former patients of mental hospitals. The facility is funded to provide traning and other services that are required to facilitate the integration of former mental hospital patients into the community. The development of work skills and successful employment is the key to reducing the recidivism rate (that is, returning to hospitals).

The agency has a budget of about $2 million. About $1.25 million is in the form of government grants. The rest comes from sales of the agency's products and services. Since the amount of the government grants is fixed, expansion of the program can occur only through an increase in the revenue from the sale of products and services.

Most clients are referred to Independence Workshop by professionals in various human service organizations. An intake worker assesses the eligibility of clients for the program by determining the likelihood of their fitting into the workshop environment and benefiting from its services. If a client is considered eligible, he or she is given aptitude tests to facilitate the assignment of work tasks.

The major thrust of the program is the actual work that clients are expected to do under close supervision. Expectations are that clients would behave in much the same way at the workshop as they would in a regular work environment. This is important — for them to develop recognized work habits (such as arriving on time, concentrating on tasks, demonstrating initiative, and cooperating with others) as well as specific work skills they could transfer to employment in the community. The objective is to have clients gainfully employed in the community, thereby becoming self-supporting. Considerable attention is paid to avoiding clients becoming dependent on a sheltered or protected work environment.

Many clients require counseling services to resolve problems affecting their performance at the workshop and their functioning in the community. Problems sometimes reflect difficulties in interpersonal relations in a work environment in which there is pressure to produce or personal and family difficulties, inadequate living conditions, and lack of money. Clients are free to visit the social workers for such counseling services. If the staff at the workshop feel a person requires counseling, the service is initiated by the social worker.

The workshop has a placement service to help locate jobs for people leaving the program. The placement service is continually attempting to identify available positions. Contacts are made with employers to make them receptive to the hiring of former mental patients.

The clients are paid a nominal hourly wage for their work. The aim is to have them recognize that they are compensated for the work they produce. For most clients, this wage is a form of welfare payments that they receive from the government.

The funding organizations judge this program according to its success in increasing the employability of clients. For this reason, the range of services is really directed toward this particular objective.

WORK EXPERIENCE PROGRAM[2]

Alarmed by the rising cost of welfare and Medicaid, the governor of Massachusetts initiated the Massachusetts Work Experience Program (MASSWEP) in January 1978 to increase the employability of welfare fathers who had been out of work for a long time and were disadvantaged on this account in finding a job. Operating through the federal-state Work Incentive Program, MASSWEP spent nearly $500,000 over 15 months in selecting and placing welfare fathers in temporary (13-week) jobs in government and other nonprofit organizations within the state. Of more than 5000 men expected to be eligible (i.e., judged to be employable but unable to find a job without assistance), some 1000 were eventually placed, for varying periods of time. Their families continued to receive welfare benefits of $350 per month, but their pay was an additional $30 per month.

On the average MASSWEP clients were in their early thirties, had ten years schooling, had held their last job for four years, and had been unemployed for more than two years. More than 90 percent had been separated from their last jobs for reasons beyond their control — e.g. fired, job disappeared, ill-health. They were predominantly white and the fathers of two children on the average. Latest jobs included a wide range of industries and occupations. Long unemployment had resulted a loss of self-esteem and a perceived handicap in job hunting because prospective employers would tend to rate them low on experience.

Participation in MASSWEP was voluntary; it was not a "workfare" program requiring welfare fathers to work for their welfare payments, although it had originally been conceived as

such. Men were initially nominated for MASSWEP if they had
been: (1) unemployed for at least six months, (2) registered with
the Work Incentive Program for at least three months, (3)
referred unsuccessfully to regular jobs or jobs under the Comprehensive Employment and Training Act, and (4) judged unsuitable for referral to an alternative component of the Work
Incentive Program.

Following initial nomination, candidates were interviewed
for assessment of their suitability for assignment to one of the
work sites promoted and established by program personnel. A
candidate could be considered unsuitable for work experience
if a physical or emotional problem warranted exemption from
the Work Incentive Program, if he first needed medical or
social services (e.g., alcoholism problems), if other Work Incentive Components might be more appropriate given his
needs, or if he needed to be referred for vocational rehabilitation. Lastly, a judgment had to be made that the lack of recent
work experience was inhibiting his reemployment.

Once into MASSWEP, the fathers were to work at their
assigned sites for up to 24 hours per week, usually three days,
and to spend the rest of the time looking for a regular job. They
were mostly in low-skill occupations of different kinds, often
tailored to their particular needs. In addition to the $30 monthly
incentive payment, the fathers also received expenses for
travel and lunches while on the sites. If they did not find a job
within the 13-week basic period, they might be given a second
similar treatment.

Overall objective: to increase full-time regular employment
among the welfare fathers with a consequent reduction in state
welfare payments.

A DIVERSION PROJECT IN THE
JUVENILE JUSTICE SYSTEM[3]

Under the leadership of the Chief Probation Officer of
Orange County, California, the Community Services Project
(CSP) was instituted in 1971 to find new ways of dealing with
increasing crime and its associated costs of crime prevention,
law enforcement, adjudication, probation and the like. The
project was launched in two cities: Fountain Valley (new and
growing) and Placentia (more stable, pioneer-based).

One of CSP's 30-odd efforts to deal with crime prevention and treatment of youthful offenders in the juvenile justice system was Alternative Routes (AR). The general purpose of the project was to develop an effective supplement to the traditional juvenile justice system by enjoining the community, its social agents, and its youth, schools, police, and probation to work together with youthful offenders.

Probation officers trained in counseling were placed in the two cities. They provided counseling and guidance to youth who were referred to the project by police, schools, parents, or neighbors, or by self-referral after having committed inappropriate acts. Referrals by police and schools were made as an alternative to other options such as probation and the courts.

Unlike their counterparts in the Probation Department, the AR workers had small caseloads and intensive contact with the AR clients, their families, and other significant members of the community. The AR workers were capable of responding immediately to requests for assistance. In comparison with the traditional system, the AR workers had considerably more interface with representatives of the police and the schools and other agencies concerned about the youthful offenders.

The workers were conveniently located in the community. Their setting was less bureaucratic than the county probation office and other agencies of the criminal justice system. Still, they continued to carry their probation badges and thus did not entirely shed their probation image.

Included in the long-range objectives of the project was the desire to develop and demonstrate an approach to treating youthful offenders while they remained in the community. Such treatment was to be (1) less costly than the more traditional approaches employed, (2) satisfactory from the youths' and families' perspectives, (3) useful from the perspectives of the leaders of key community institutions like police and schools, and (4) effective in reducing recidivism among those treated.

Specific commitments were established for each funding year (the program was funded mainly by grants from the Law Enforcement Assistance Administration):

(1) To provide alternative services for 280 young people who would have normally been referred by police, probation, parents, or schools to the formal juvenile justice system.

(2) To provide treatment and diagnostic services to 500 young people and their families who were in need of service but who would not receive assistance from the present system.

(3) To provide group counseling in conjunction with school officials to assist 100 young people with personal, home, and school problems.

(4) To provide education and information to 300 students regarding drug abuse, delinquency, law, the Juvenile Court, and individuals' rights and responsibilities.

(5) To reduce by one to five weeks the time between an incident of socially dysfunctional behavior and the commencement of a treatment or rehabilitation program in all cases that formerly would have been referred to the formal juvenile justice system.

THE ATLANTA ADOLESCENT PREGNANCY PROGRAM[4]

The Atlanta Adolescent Pregnancy Program (AAPP) was organized under the auspices of the Maternity and Infant Care Project in Atlanta. The three-year program was initiated in 1968 to provide comprehensive health, educational, and social services to all pregnant students in two Atlanta high schools. It proposed to develop innovative methods for delivery of health care and other services, and to effect permanent changes in the delivery of social services of many social and health agencies in Atlanta.

Specific AAPP objectives were to increase the number of pregnant young women who stayed in school, to decrease unwanted pregnancies, to decrease the rates of premature births and prenatal and infant mortality, to improve the opportunities of the girl and infant to establish a stable family life, to demonstrate the feasibility of regular high school as an option for the girl, and to render services to all pregnant and postpartum students in the program schools.

Under the AAPP, 341 pregnant girls, nearly all from low-income, nonwhite families, in two Atlanta high schools remained in classes and related extracurricular activities during pregnancy and after childbirth. Not only were special classes in nutrition, health, and family life provided during the pregnancy, but special tutoring, aided by programmed instruction, was also arranged for during the postpartum hospital stay.

At her entrance into the program, each adolescent was

evaluated, and a two-year postpartum program arranged for her, involving all the appropriate services with which the AAPP had contact in the community. Health care was provided, including health examinations, and special exercise courses were taught in the high school. Special family planning services were provided for AAPP clients. Every AAPP worker was thoroughly informed on family planning methods so that any girl's questions could be answered without referring her to another clinic. An important service of the AAPP was the special counseling given to the father by male workers, which primarily involved helping him find a job or continue his education.

In addition to these services, the AAPP attempted to integrate and coordinate existing community resources (such as free lunches and groups willing to donate infants' clothing), to provide day care (a difficult problem), to train personnel from the two high schools who were assisting in AAPP-sponsored classes (by means of postgraduate courses and seminars), to follow up the individuals served by the program and to undertake community education.

After discussing the reasons usually given for separating the expectant adolescent from her peers in school, the AAPP report proposes that such action is a denial of her civil rights and that legislation is needed to clarify this. On the basis of its own experience, the AAPP hypothesizes that about 80 percent of its pregnant adolescents can continue successfully in school. One of the benefits of the proposal to the school system is that it eliminates the exorbitant expense of forming "special schools." It was recommended that special schools, if used at all, be established for pregnant girls in grammar school.

NOTES

1. Prepared by Dr. Leonard Rutman for graduate course work in program evaluation, School of Social Work, Carleton University, Ottawa.

2. Barry Friedman, Barbara Davenport, Robert Evans, Andrew Hahn, Leonard Hausman, and Cecile Papirno, *An Evaluation of the Massachusetts Work Experience Program* (Washington, DC: U.S. Department of Health and Human Services, 1980). Some data have been modified for this program summary.

3. G. Ronald Gilbert, "Alternative Routes: A Diversion Project in the Juvenile Justice System," *Evaluation Quarterly 1* (May 1977): 301-303.

4. *Research to Improve Health Services for Mothers and Children* (Washington, DC: U.S. Department of Health, Education and Welfare, May 1973). DHEW Publication (HSM) 73-5116.

ABOUT THE AUTHORS

LEONARD RUTMAN is Professor in the School of Social Work at Carleton University and a consultant to Price Waterhouse Associates. He received his BA and MSW at the University of Manitoba and his Ph. D. from the University of Minnesota. He has previously taught in the Sociology Department at the University of Winnipeg. He has consulted extensively for several departments in the provincial and federal governments in Canada and has done some work for UNESCO. He is author of *Planning Useful Evaluations: Evaluability Assessment,* and co-author (with Dick de Jong) of *Federal Level Evaluation* (1976) and (with Andrew Jones) of *In the Children's Aid: J.J. Kelso and Child Welfare Reform in Ontario* (1980). Rutman also edited *Drugs: Use and Abuse* (1969) and *Evaluation Research Methods: A Basic Guide* (1977).

GEORGE MOWBRAY is President of the Management Planning Institute, Toronto and Ottawa. An economist, sociologist, and writer, he has had a longstanding interest in the practical problems of program management and training in the public sector. In addition to articles and reports on economics, management planning, government policy, and legislative auditing, his books include, *Underwriting Canadian Health* and *The Economic Impact of Colleges and Universities on the Boston Area.*